VIKINGOLOGY·ACCORDING·TO·HASSAN·SØRENSEN

VIKINGOLOGY ACCORDING TO HASSAN SØRENSEN

2023 TEXT, LAYOUT AND GRAPHIC BY THE MIGHTY WRITER AND GRAPHIC DESIGNER
HASSE "HASSAN" SØRENSEN

COVER PHOTO BY VLASTIMIL ŠESTÁK

PUBLISHED BY PROPAGANDAMINISTERIET
PRINTED BY INGRAMSPARK™

ISBN: 978-87-974024-8-1

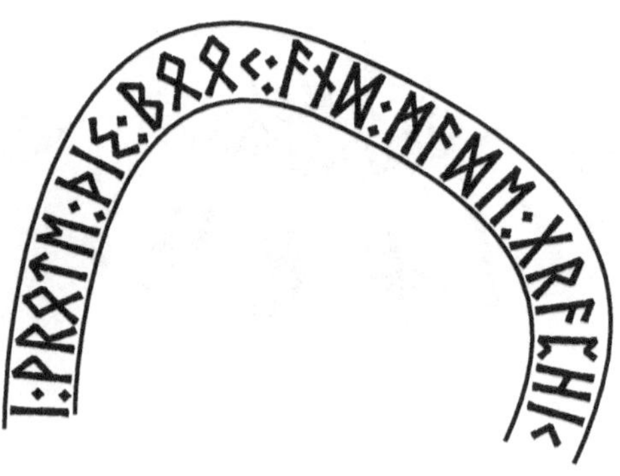

CONTENT

ᚠᛏᚹ:ᛖᛉ:ᛁᛏ:ᛒᛖᚷᛁᛏᛖ

VIKINGOLOGY

While reading this book I highly recommend you listen to the album *"Vedergällningen"* by Garmana.

Most words and names you don't recognise will be explained in the Encyclopedia parts of the book.

Scandinavian letters:

Ä/Æ/ä/æ = Like E in *"Elf"*.

Ö/Ø/ö/ø = Pronounced almost like the Ea in *"Earth"*.

Å/å = Almost like Oa *"Oar"*.

Ð / ð = Soft D, almost like TH in *"Heathen"* (Tip of tongue behind front teeth).

Þ/ þ = Soft T, like Th in *"thing"* (Þorvald ≈ Thorvald) (Tip of tongue below front teeth).

I will write names as close to the original as possible. Find alternate spellings in the Encyclopedia part of the book.

When I mention Iron Age Vikings – or Vikings in past tense – I mean Iron Age and early mediaeval times, c.300-c.1300.

I mention *"central Sweden"* as the origin of the Rus, but technically speaking the area around lake Mälaren is still southern Sweden – just a little further north than the Dane's *"southern Sweden"*, as Sweden now stretches all the way up to north of the polar circle.

What is missing from this book is 2500 times the word *"presumably"*, 500 times *"probably"* and 200 times *"I believe"*.

Tomorrow an archaeological dig will reveal everything in this book to be thoroughly wrong.

ALL·THE·ANSWERS

ATTACK!

One moment it's quiet, the sun is shining from a partly cloudy sky, and if you listen carefully you can hear a blackbird singing its beautiful and intricate tune. There's a mild breeze making the heat bearable.

Suddenly there's a loud unpleasant roar, and over the top of the hill a group of Vikings with round shields, raised axes, and fearless faces advances, like an unstoppable force of death and severed limbs.

The sunlight is reflected in their helmets, your chest is tightening so much it almost brings your heart to a stop, and your throat goes dry, while the dust swirls up around you.

You can almost taste the blood in the air.

Over the roar you hear the recognisable sound of an iPhone ringing.

The attack loses some of its stamina, and a voice is heard: *"Knuð, for helveðe...".*

You have been the innocent victim of a Viking reenactment.

Why are Scandinavians still fetishizing the Iron Age?

How come this particular period in history shaped the Scandinavian identity?

Let's find out!

MODERN VIKINGS

If you go to Scandinavia you will find yourself in the middle of the Viking Age.
You might not see it at first, maybe even shake your head and think *"nonsense – that was a long time ago"*.
Slowly you will start noticing the slightly odd behaviour, the weird names and the ever present Iron Age grave mounts. You will start seeing Mjölnir, Jǫrmungandr, Yggdrasil and fuþart everywhere. Suddenly you can't stop seeing it. Sooner or later it will dawn on you: *It's not over yet.*

Relax. We don't desecrate altars, burn monasteries and enslave monks anymore. We have found more subtle ways to express our general lack of consideration.

A defining part of Viking culture is a fair amount of insensitivity and a merciless rationality.
If public hugging and kissing, breastfeeding and giraffe autopsies are too much for you, and religious satire makes you angry, you will consider us barbaric.

Yet you will find the Scandinavian countries at the top of the list whenever development is ranked; happiness, education, equality, atheism, healthcare, work-life-balance, social security and sustainable energy.
The World Economic Forum and United Nations annual reports look suspiciously like Scandinavian fanmail.

We don't discriminate by *innate* characteristics (such as gender, skin colour or sexual orientation), while *choices* (faiths and opinions) are always subject to debate and ridicule, in words and artistic expressions.

Perhaps the most defining ability of Vikings is *adaptability*, which is how we transitioned from Forn Siðr through

Christianity to atheism, from fuþark (runes) to the Latin alphabet, and from villains to virtue, without losing our specific character on the journey.

It happens, once in a while, some actually get offended by our lack of consideration. Rest assured you are welcome to burn our flag, the bible and constitution, and even a picture of the queen.
No harm done, as no one is physically inconvenienced.

All things considered, we are still Vikings.

Viking is *not* an ethnicity, a religion or a membership club. It's something subtle and indefinable in the culture and the landscape, and it affects us; even those whose grandparents immigrated from somewhere else, and the ones whose knowledge of history is shockingly deficient and flawed.

My youngest daughter's daycare centre was named Midgården, her classmates had names like Erik, Harald and Astrið, and she learned what I have learned, and what her children will learn: The thunder is Þhórr (Thor) acting out with his hammer, Mjölnir.
She names everything, like her iPhone, bicycle, potted plants and jewellery.
Her grandmother used to wear a Mjölnir necklace, even to church. Not to provoke, but it's so common here, nobody gives it a second thought.
Grandma's dead now, so we will light candles in front of a runestone.

In December 2021 I was invited to make an exhibition in the centre of Copenhagen, with the title *"Imagine Modern Vikings"*. The idea was to imagine what Denmark would have looked like, had the Iron Age Vikings been more culturally conservative.

A lot of research and some photoshopping. The more re-search we did, the more pointless it became.
Being conservative would have been self-contradictory for an Iron Age Scandinavian. After all, their success was driven by plasticity.
You don't have to imagine modern Vikings; just look around. It's right here, right now.

Only a few Scandinavians will put *"Viking"* on their business card or Facebook profile, but they will still refer to Kristmesse (Christmas) as *"Jul"*, and talk about Þórr when they hear the thunder.

It's inescapable.

The Christian cross dominates all the Scandinavian flags, but you will not find many believers. Neither will you find any other countries with a higher percentage of female and/or homosexual priests.

Obviously we don't actually believe in Æsir and Tróls either, but they are – nevertheless – everywhere, all the time.

WHAT THE F... IS A VIKING?

August 9th 2021 I got on the wrong train and ended up in Växjö.

While waiting for a train to get me back on track, I took a walk around the nearby church.

At the back of the church I saw a rune stone, and posted it on Instagram, as you do.

On this runestone, the author refers to himself as a Viking.

Many historians' favourite statement is: *"They didn't call themselves Vikings!"*

Some did, apparently.

In the European runestone database (www.runesdb.eu) it's runestone number [SM10], and there are more.

No one knows for sure where the word comes from. It could be Viken, the area around Oslo; it can be robbers (as in the Anglo-Saxon chronicle that says *"They came as Vikings"*); it can be expedition (*"He died in viking, on the western route"* [VG 61]); or it can simply mean Scandinavian.

The common modern meaning is: All Scandinavians, in the Viking Age.

This gets twisted a bit here, because elsewhere in the book I argue that the Viking Age is not over.

So Vikings are people from Iceland, the Faroe Islands, the Shetland Islands, Denmark, Sweden, Norway and southern Finland.

The Viking concept has been derailed time and time again by racists, therapists, insecure men, scientists, fortune tellers, fitness fanatics and Marvel Comics.

In popular culture, Vikings are portrayed as tall, blond, muscular, bloodthirsty, tattooed rapists who yearn to die in battle so they can get to Valhalla.

Equipped with a long sword, a large round shield and horns in the helmet.

The reality is a little different, even in the historical Viking Age (approx. 300 - 1350).

Some were tall, as the diet was rather healthy and nutritious in Scandinavia.

A very few were blonde, and the number increased as people immigrated (more or less voluntarily) from Eastern Europe.

There was an immigration and emigration of about 25% per generation during the Iron Age.

According to modern DNA analyses, there are most likely twice as many blonde people in Scandinavia now as in the Iron Age.

Most of the people who worked in the fields ten hours a day, without mechanical aids, were probably muscular.

The Vikings were hyper violent, in a hyper violent age.

Like so many others, they used the tactic that the first raids were a veritable bloodbath, the chief of the town or the high priest of the monastery was tortured to death while people watched, everything was looted, and the town or monastery burned down. A few were allowed to escape, while the rest were killed or taken as slaves.

The effect was that the next time the Vikings approached a town, the inhabitants would pay large sums – so-called *"Danegæld"* – to make them disappear.

Sources suggest that some Rus Vikings were tattooed, while the Danes were not.

In general, most people tried to keep themselves and their families alive as long as possible. The desire to get to Valhalla – or rather Folkvangr – was probably not as pronounced as it has become in popular culture.

A few people from the upper classes used a long sword, but most used tools from the farm and the hunt: the axe and the bow.

The large round shield is one of the few things that actually hits the mark.

If you go into a souvenir shop and buy a Viking figurine, it has horns in its helmet. It's simple iconography – that's how we recognize a Viking.

We know they didn't have horns in their helmets, so where does that idea come from?

At the Bayreuther Festspiele's production of Wagner's *"Der Ring des Nibelungen"*, in 1876, scenographer Carl Emil Doepler wanted Brunhilde to look more terrifying. He took some drinking horns from the stage and glued them to her helmet.

It was Carl's idea, *"made in Germany"*.

The Vikings were in fact a large, motley group of ordinary people who wanted to survive and thrive under the given circumstances: farmers, craftsmen, merchants, warriors, slave traders, etc.

At the end of the 7th century, the Great Nordic Expansion started, where raids increased and the search started for new agricultural land.

The Danes went west, while the Rus went east.

Their success is primarily due to three factors: Cleanliness, good ships and readiness for change.

Unaware of viruses and bacteria, Iron Age Scandinavians developed a penchant for washing themselves and their children, which made people live longer and better, and more babies survive.

The unique ship design made the boats light, durable, flexible and suitable for both crossing the ocean and sailing into rivers and lakes.

Rationality made them more adaptable in almost all situations.

Since the culture was based on traditions rather than institutions, there were no consequences when they allied with Picts, Frisians or Slavic peoples, converted to Christianity or sold white slaves to Africans.

Their success is therefore due to the fact that they were not fanatical nationalists, religious or ethnocentric.

Valdemar was born in Birka, blessed by the Asers, and 60 years later was given a Christian burial in Kiev as Vladimir.

This is a typical Viking story.

Christians fought each other with all means, but would rarely attack a monastery, and therefore the monasteries had almost no defences. For some Vikings, this was a niche they could exploit.

We are therefore talking about well-groomed, rational people, completely devoid of inhibitions.

In the first half of the historical Viking Age, most people were æsir-believers (forn Siðr – the old customs), and in the second half many had converted to Christianity (Inn nýí siðr – the new customs).

Rationality and integrity are still central values for Vikings, and everyone has everything at home to cope with any situation: Sewing machine, drill, drawing materials, a well-equipped toolbox, hobby equipment…

Even an axe.

For other peoples, it seems strange, and some of my friends from, for example, Southeast Asia are confused: *"Why do you have all that shit?"*

We don't attack churches anymore, so the fearlessness is reduced to leaving one's laptop on a café table when we go to the restroom, or leaving our babies in the pram out on the pavement.

Primitive and barbaric madness in the eyes of many others.

WHEN WAS THE VIKING AGE?

It's vital to note the Viking Age is a fabrication.

The term first appeared on the cover of the booklet *"The Dane's Culture in the Viking Age"* by Jens Jacob Asmussen Worsaae in 1873.

Nobody has ever thought themselves to be living in the Viking Age.

So we are discussing the beginning and perhaps the end of a period that is a *fabrication*; there are no right or wrong answers, only opinions.

According to Professor Lene Melheim, at the Museum of Cultural History in Oslo, it began 500 BC – and maybe sooner – as petroglyphs reveal Viking expeditions in the Bronze Age.

According to the Anglo-Saxon Chronicle it began June 8th 793 AD, with the attack on Lindisfarne monastery.

As the only written source the Anglo-centric narrative gets a lot of attention, however irrelevant it may be.

Archaeologists are finding earlier and earlier manifestations of the Viking ship design, and traces of earlier and earlier trading and raiding farther and farther away.

It's extremely difficult to set a date, or even a century, and say: *"This is where it began"*.

To have any kind of reference I will set the year 300, where Uppsala was established.

But I could have chosen any other year, without being wrong or right.

That was the easy part.

The hard part is telling when it ended – or ends.

Valdemar is born in Uppsala, blessed by the ásynja Freyja, and sixty years later Vladimir gets a Christian burial in Kievan Rus. That is perhaps the most typical Viking story.

He moves around, rises to the challenge and changes with the circumstances.

Being Viking means being open-minded, curious, adaptable and rational.

It's pretty hard establishing an end date for such a phenomenon.

Maybe it ended with the christening of the Scandinavian population; a process that technically speaking took 650 years from the first mission in Ribe to the last major Blót festival in Sweden. In reality it's not fulfilled yet.

That would be a daft and very vague definition.

Maybe it ended with the death of Haraldr *"Harðráði"* Sigurðarson, at the battle of Stamford Bridge, in 1066. But at that point Kievan Rus (also known as Garðaríki) was peaking, and the Varangian Guard was recruiting Vikings by the shiploads.

Maybe it ended when they stopped sailing... Wait a minute: The (by far) largest shipping company in the world is Mærsk, from the micronation of Denmark.

Besides the raiding and pillaging, Vikings invented *Altinget*, the modern parliament, a key component of modern representative democracy. I could argue when that ends it's the end of the Viking Age.

It's really not that easy, and tomorrow you will still be able to recognise that weird Viking attitude in Scandinavia.

We can argue for hours about this, but at the end of the day, in a shady pub in Reykjavik, I dare you to say out loud *"The Viking Age is over!"*

I will say it's *not*, and whoever comes out alive wins the argument.

VIKING BELIEFS

As far back in time we can trace the Scandinavians – and everyone else a few thousand kilometres in every direction, including Germanic tribes, Kelts, Picts, Saxons and Sámis – worshipped a number of Æsir (deities).

Æsir are not to be confused with Gods, as they are mortal, even if they live for thousands of years, and hold magic powers.

Like the Greek and Roman deities they have human flaws and quirks, and tales about mischiefs and fuckups we can learn from.

Unlike the Mediterranean deities they don't have specific personal functions. For war, love or harvest, different varied groups of Æsir will stand in line to receive blót (offerings and prayers) and offer their assistance.

Freyja is dedicated to love and sex, but in times of war she will mount the boar Hildisvíni and ride into battle.

As we move from the Stone Age into the Bronze Age, and onwards, the pantheon grows, and the belief turns more complicated.

There are Æsir and Vanir, Light Elves and Black Elves, Jotunn, Tróls and Nisser.

The interchanging relations – and interbreeding – between them suggests they are not different species, kinds or races, but rather different nations, inhabiting different spheres or dimensions, placed around the world tree Yggdrasil.

Obviously local editions of this belief would vary enormously.

It's vitally important to remember this is tradition, not a homogeneous institutionalised religion.

It didn't have a name, a book, a hierarchy of bishops and priests, or even a consensus.

When it finally got a name – or label – it was *"Forn Siðr"* (the old ways), but only as opposed to *"Inn nyí siðr"* (the new ways – Christianity).

Today it is primarily known as ásstrú (Æsir-belief).

Most would acknowledge Óðinn as the main Æsir – the Allfather – while others would place the new kid in the block, Þórr, in the middle.

There are no traces of Þórr in the Bronze Age, but in the Iron Age he becomes vitally important, and his War hammer Mjölnir becomes a token for identification, just like the cross is used by Christians.

From around year 600 Christianity comes creeping in, and a rising number of people add Jesus to their pantheon.

Yeah… It's *Jesus* – *"Hvítakristr"* – not *God*, as a disembodied God would have been a ridiculously hard sell to the Vikings.

In 700 many neighbouring countries were already more or less Christian, and the first known Scandinavian church was built in Ribe.

In the coming centuries it becomes important to identify as a Christian, in order to travel and trade in the areas outside the Vikings dominance.

Around the year 1000 most Viking lands are officially proclaimed Christian, though large Blót festivals are still going on in central Sweden until at least the 1350s.

Getting the Vikings to add Jesus Christ to their pantheon was the easy part, however, as it turns out to be much more gruelling to make them abandon the Æsir and Forn Siðr.

It's worth noticing the mediaeval Catholic Church is quite a mouthful, with many rules, several annual periods of fasting, and rather extreme misogyny.

Forn Siðr, that is a loose tradition, does not try to repel Christianity, while the Christian missionaries have a slightly strained relationship with polytheism.

Many compromises later, in the 1500's, the Scandinavian countries jumped on the Lutheran trend, and bid the Catholic Church and the Pope farewell.

I'm confident he was kind of relieved.

In modern times basic education obviously starts pushing religion aside, and the atrocities during World War ll is the last nail in the coffin.

Maybe best explained by citing a graffiti found in Mauthausen concentration camp: *"If there is a God he will have to beg for my forgiveness"*.

In all the Scandinavian countries it is common to be a member of the national Lutheran church (65%), be baptised (50%), married (30%) and buried (65%) aided by the church, while being a *de facto* atheist.

These numbers are dropping fast.

This is all driven by tradition, and nobody will go to church without a specific occasion.

In Denmark confirmation has become a huge thing, and teenagers get baptised in order to participate in confirmation, which has become bigger (and more expensive!) than weddings. This has nothing to do with faith, and it hasn't spread to the other Scandinavian countries.

Especially in Sweden the church is now trying to catch up with modernity, by marketing the *"Rainbow Church"*, but not with a lot of success.

Forn Siðr is an officially recognised religion, but caters to a very small number of members, in spite of trying to modernise in much the same way.

Note there is a whole part of this book dedicated to the mythologies of Forn Siðr, Christianity and Islam.

NETFLIX VIKINGS

Is there any truth to the History Channel/Netflix TV series "Vikings"?

[Spoiler alert]

Painting with a broad brush I would say *"yes, definitely!"*.

What is important to understand is that the skilled writers – Michael Hirst in particular – had to work with the same material as historians and museums around the world: Archaeological excavations without manifests, fragments of highly questionable mediaeval chronicles, weird fantasy sagas, and incoherent stories about mostly legendary people.

They didn't have the luxury of saying *"this is open for interpretation"*.

They had to tear the fragments further apart, and stitch together a coherent, catching and exciting storyline, introducing a manageable number of characters.

They did, however, have the luxury of saying *"this doesn't have to be historically accurate"*, so they could move people, events and time around to fit the narrative.

That Hrólfr (Rollo) in fact wasn't born until fifty years after the Lindisfarne raid, that the Sámi princess Snøfrid Svåsedottir was in fact married to Haraldr Hárfagri (Harald Finehair), and that the Viking jumping out of his coffin in fact happened a hundred years later in Italy, is just a slight distortions, made to give you a story worth watching and following.

I wouldn't want them to change a thing, and I applaud them for doing the same as Snorri Sturluson, Saxo Grammaticus, and all other saga writers have done: Reinterpret, retell and give me a good story.

That's the Scandinavian way.

Lagerþa and Ragnarr *"Loðbrók"* Sigurðsson are legendary – presumably fictitious – characters from the sagas, and by the time they raided Lindisfarne monastery Vikings had been going to England for hundreds of years – everybody knew where it was, and the sun stone and water compass was well known by everybody.

At that time, human sacrifice was just a vague memory of an ancient past.

But that's not exciting.

They have managed to present Iron Age Scandinavian culture in a semi-relatable way, catering to modern trends (like tattoos), and they have been forced to use their uttermost imagination to create the scary and weird Forn Siðr priests.

Obviously I could spend several hours and pages picking this story apart, but I would end up with thousands of incoherent and questionable fragments, and no story to tell.

Could I tell a better story, closer to the truth? Definitely not.

I would end up with thousands of gaps, and hundreds of *"Sliding Doors"*-like situations where we could experience different versions of the same events.

Furthermore I would have to introduce a bewildering number of new characters, making you profoundly confused.

Some day, in the future, another screenwriter will dive into the rabbit hole with one of these characters, and tell a different story that will contradict this TV series – and everything is as it has always been.

WHERE DID THE VIKINGS COME FROM, AND WHERE DID THEY GO?

There were a number of groups that can be distinguished: The Danes, the Svea, the Goutar and the Gotar. To simplify this I will put the Svea, Goutar and Gotar in one group, as they are also collectively known as the Rus.

So: Danes and Rus.

(My dead body will be found in a ditch because of this simplification, I know. That's okay.)

Besides them there are two other groups in Scandinavia that are not commonly labelled Vikings, as they have rather different cultures and languages, and mostly stayed at home: The Finns and the Sámi.

The Danes lived in the south western part of present day Norway, all of present day Denmark, a small part of northern Germany and the southernmost part of Sweden.

Between Norway and Sweden there's a mountain range, and from the southernmost part of Sweden to central Sweden is a forested area of completely worthless farmland, today's Småland. These barriers divided the Danes from the Rus, and made the contact between the two groups sparse (according to recent DNA studies).

In the years of the *"Great Norse Expansion"* (c.800-c.1100) the Danes ventured west, to Holland, Belgium, France, England, Scotland, Ireland, Shetland Islands, Faroe Islands, Iceland, Greenland and Canada.

The Rus went east, to Finland, Estonia, Russia, Belarus, Ukraine, Romania, Bulgaria, Turkey, Iran and Iraq.

Obviously none of these countries existed at that time.

They had been exploring, trading and raiding in parts of these areas since the 600s or 700s, some places since the Bronze Age, and some since the Stone Age, but now they started settling and occupying territory.

Were the Vikings "Explorers" or "Exploiters"?

From c.700 definitely exploiters!

RAIDERS

Before the expansion both Danes and Rus travelled west and east, respectively, to trade, raid, explore and exploit.

Many countries, especially to the west, were Christian, and even if they had disputes and fought each other vigorously, they would never dare raid a church – *"the house of God"*.

The Vikings observed that, and found a profitable niche.

They didn't have total monopoly on this niche, however, and even groups of Christians have been known to raid churches and monasteries, on occasions.

The Vikings raiders were ultra violent, in an ultra violent world, and many of the slaves they took were actually already slaves to other masters. So it was slave-stealing.

This is not to whitewash the Viking raiders, as they were definitely assholes, but to say: So was everybody else, at that time.

THE DANES

For the Danes, who went west, it was mostly a hunt for good farmland.

In England they established themselves in Jórik (York), and with constantly changing alliances and both internal and external fighting they gained and lost land, to the point where it is completely impossible to keep track.

In the year 865 they managed to cooperate for the creation of the so-called *"Great Heathen Army"*. The result was Danelagen, which literally means the area where the Dane's law applies.

That was a small part of Scotland and all of England, except for Wessex in the south and a part of Wales.

In Ireland they made a few minor camps, before founding Dublin in 841, as a major trading harbour, primarily for the slave trade.

The river Seine in present day France attracted many Viking raiders, who plundered monasteries and marked towns, until the Frankish king made a deal with one of them.

Hrólfr (Rollo) was given the area around the river mouth, for the establishment of Normandy. This way he would act as a buffer between raiding Vikings and Frankia.

Others ventured north, to the Shetland Islands and the Faroe Islands.

According to sagas Naddoðr discovered a new island in the north Atlantic, found it uninteresting, named it Snow Island, and hurried back to the Faroe Island.

Learning this *"Hrafna"*-Flóki Vilgerðarson gathers a group of people and sailed off to populate this uninhabited island.

When this attempt failed completely he renamed Snow Island to Iceland, and left.

The next attempt, in 860, was successful.

Naddoðr's great great grandson Þorvald Ásvaldsson killed a man in Norway. For that he was exiled, and moved with his family to Iceland.

In Iceland his son – now a grown man – Eiríkur *"Rauði"* Þorvaldsson (Erik the Red) killed a man.

(This is beginning to look like a pattern.)

For that he was exiled, and ventures north to find a place to live.

In 981 he discovered Greenland.

Five years later he returned to Greenland with a larger group of Icelanders and created Brattalið, a settlement with a trading station.

There had been a small number of walrus in Iceland, providing the settlers with valuable ivory, but they were long gone. In Greenland the walrus was plentiful, along with sealskin and other precious goods.

The same year, 986, Bjarni Herjólfsson was blown off course in an attempt to sail from Iceland to Greenland. When he finally found land it didn't match the description of Greenland at all, and he turned the boat around to get on the right course.

His description of these unknown shores had quite an effect when he told the story in Greenland.

Greenland has no trees, and *"trees as tall as mountains"* made the ship building Greenlanders very interested.

There are no descriptions of investigative expeditions, but there must have been some.

In year 1000 two of Eiríkur's children, Leifur *"Heppni"* Eiríksson (Leif the Happy) and Freydís Eiríksdóttir lead the establishment of a settlement in Vinland (perhaps L'Anse aux Meadows in present day Canada).

Until this the Vikings going north had found unpopulated lands. Vinland was, however, populated, and even though their garbage disposal reveals they have moved quite a lot around, as far as present day New York, the settlement was given up after only 15 years.

This has been thought to be the end of the story, but there were probably a number of later expeditions from Greenland to fetch timber.

In 1347 Icelandic documents record that a ship ended up in Iceland when returning from Markland (somewhere in the Labrador coast in Canada).

While all this was going on, in the 900s, other Danes travelled south, along the European coastline, and into the Mediterranean, for trading and raiding.

As they came to the end of the Mediterranean sea they arrived in Miklagarðr (Constantinople, present day Istanbul), where they met the Rus – old friends from back home.

THE RUS

The Rus come from the area around lake Mälaren in present day Sweden. The important city of Uppsala was established as early as 300 AD, and the important cities Birka and Sigtuna were established around the year 700, near present day Stockholm.

From Birka they went across the Baltic Sea, and found the river mouth to the Dnieper river, which took them all the way to Miklagarðr.

A shopping trip of 2,700 kilometres through partly hostile territory.

In Miklagarðr they could sell amber, exotic Scandinavian fur, white slaves and high quality steel.

In return they could get silver, gold, precious stones, silk, and other exciting goods from Africa and Asia, as Miklagarðr was at the end of the silk road.

The voyage along the Dnieper river was not entirely safe, though, as the Pechenegs and other groups of Slavic people would rob them at any given chance.

In 862 Hrøríkr (Rurik) established a fortress in Holmgarðr (Novgorod) to protect the trade.

In 879 his brother (ruling on behalf of Hrøríkr's young son) moved this power centre to Kyiv.

By controlling the areas around both the Dnieper and the Volga rivers the Kievan Rus empire became a reality.

In 941 Rus Vikings besieged Miklagarðr with some success, though they never penetrated the city wall.

In 944 they did it again, and this time they got a favourable trade agreement, and the Byzantine emperor was so impressed with their fighting skills he created an elite unit of Viking mercenaries called the Varangian Guard.

"Varangian" was the Byzantine name for the Vikings.

As a result of this arrangement Rus Vikings now continued on to places like Babylon and Baghdad.

The Vikings didn't mint coins themselves, but as silver coins held a real value they were usable as payment everywhere in the world. For that reason both coins from the Byzantine empire and the Abbasid caliphate have been found in Viking graves as far away as England. Graves in Birka and Uppsala are almost littered with Arab Dirhams.

Recently Doctor Cat Jarman identified some semi precious stones, from a Viking grave in England, that can only be found in Gujarat, in India.

In a grave in Uppsala a Buddha statue was found, that originated in present day Afghanistan.

Hrøríkr is considered the founder of the Rurik dynasty, which went on to rule Kievan Rus' and its principalities, and ultimately the Tsardom of Russia. Vasili IV, who reigned until 1610, was the last Rurikid monarch of Russia.

Obviously the Rus gave name to both Russia and Belarus, and the Slavic population involuntarily gave name to slaves and slavery.

HOW DID THE VIKINGS DISAPPEAR?

Oh, no no, we didn't disappear. We adapted to modernity.

After 15 years the Vikings left Vinland, and in the 13th century they disappeared from Greenland, and in these cases there are lots of unanswered questions.

But in the rest of the world some went back to Scandinavia, and others simply blended into the indigenous population.

That means the population in Russia, Ukraine, Ireland, England, Scotland and Normandy (in France) have ancestors that are a mix of Vikings and locals (and slaves, and earlier and later immigrants, and… Well, it's a mess, but the Vikings blended in).

In Scandinavia, Shetland Islands, Faroe Islands and Iceland we are simply ancestors of Iron Age Vikings, blended with immigrants; the closer to mainland Europe the more mixed. Obviously.

This shows in language, customs, and to some extent in DNA.

In Iceland the mix is the least, and they have maintained patronymic last names, learning fuþark (runes) in school, and would almost(!) be able to talk to an Iron Age Dane.

One can be puzzled by the Viking's weird attraction to some very unwelcoming places, like the Shetland Islands and Greenland.

At one point they seemed to lose some of that interest.

Did they come to their senses?

It's worth noticing the climate warming up in the Scandinavian Bronze Age, and cooling significantly in the beginning of the mediaeval times.

This cooling appeared simultaneously with the Vikings disappearing from Greenland.

This could be the explanation, or part of, or it could be totally coincidental.

When Greenland started getting significantly colder Inuits moved south, where they met the Viking settlers. Archaeological excavations reveal some trading and exchange of know-how has taken place, but no finds or sagas suggest hostility or romantic relations.

So we have no reason to believe the disappearance is due to blending in, or being massacred.

In the 1700s there was a growing curiosity in Denmark-Norway about the fate of the *"Greenlanders"*, and rumours spread that their descendants were still living there.

The priest Hans Egede got the king's permission to go look for them. He didn't find them, but established a new colony in present day Nuuk, where he started converting the Inuit to Christianity. The Danish interests in Greenland was, however, neither to find surviving Vikings nor to convert Inuits, but whaling and seal skin.

Strictly speaking most Scandinavian settlers in Iceland, Faroe Islands and Greenland are of Norwegian descent, but when the union between the crowns of Denmark and Norway was dissolved in 1814, the Treaty of Kiel severed Norway's former colonies and left them under the control of the Danish monarch, with the exception of Svalbard.

Iceland became fully independent in 1944 (during World War ll), but still send university students to Denmark.

GLOBAL COOLING

In year 536 a number of major volcanic eruptions created a global cooling that left traces all over the world. It's referred to as *"three years without summer"*, and the death toll was catastrophic. It's being observed as the inspiration for the Fimbulvintr in Norse mythology.

After this event the world started warming up again, and scholars believe that the climate in the Iron Age was significantly warmer than in the *"Little Ice Age"* that began in the 1350s.

New settlements, abandoning settlements, replacement of entire communities etc. can all be explained by this factor. Large parts of the history in the Bronze Age, Iron Age and mediaeval times can be related directly to climate changes.

It basically means every time we think about a time in history it's a vital subject to take into consideration: How was the climate?

This even includes details like fashion and architecture, diet and travel routes.

In the 1300s the Vikings in Brattalið, in southern Greenland, suddenly had guests: The Inuits from central and northern Greenland moved in on their turfs, and we can see that some trading and exchange of knowledge has taken place, and in the middle of the century the Vikings disappeared from Greenland. This might be partly explained by the plague in Europe, riding them off customers, or competing ivory from Africa, or more violent events, but climate change is perhaps the most safe bet.

According to scientists we are in the opposite predicament now, and must move large cities further inland, to higher ground, which is more difficult now, as we have become more settled with concrete houses and plumbing, electrical installations, roads and so on. The Vikings in the Iron Age were slightly more versatile in their lifestyle.

The Rök stone [ÖG 136] is a famous runestone from Östergötland in Sweden, created in the first half of the 8th century and the oldest known mention of Fimbulvintr.

HOW DO WE KNOW ABOUT THE IRON AGE VIKINGS?

The Iron Age Scandinavians didn't write chronicles or even sagas, so we only have descriptions by contemporary outside observers, mediaeval Vikings, and archaeology.

It's like a 100,000 piece puzzle, and we only have 20,000 pieces.

Some of the pieces might not belong to this puzzle…

CONTEMPORARY OBSERVERS

To most of the contemporary writers the Vikings were the enemy, or at least scary strangers quite far outside the comfort zone.

We have the Anglo-Saxon Chronicles from England; chronological account of events in Anglo-Saxon and Norman England, a compilation of seven surviving interrelated manuscript records that is the primary source for the early history of England. The narrative was first assembled in the reign of King Alfred (871–899).

The authors have every reason to dislike the Viking raiders and invaders, and even their own kings for not providing sufficient protection for monasteries. That can explain why they found it necessary to include explicit details in the description of the attack on Lindisfarne monastery, and maybe even add some.

Reading the Anglo-Saxon chronicles is comparable to reading modern English tabloids; a highly unreliable source for accurate objective descriptions of actual events.

We have the Primary Chronicle from present day Ukraine, also known as *"Chronicle of Nestor"* or the *"Kiev Chronicle"*. The chronicle, compiled in Kyiv about 1113, was based on materials taken from Byzantine chronicles, west and south Slavonic literary sources, official documents, and oral sagas.

I don't believe it's necessary to explain why this source is of questionable quality.

Gesta Hammaburgensis ecclesiae pontificum (Medieval Latin for *"Deeds of the Bishops of Hamburg"*) is a historical record written between 1073 and 1076 by Adam of Bremen. It is one of the most important sources of the mediaeval history of Northern Europe, and the oldest textual source reporting the discovery of coastal North America.

As the bishops had jurisdiction over the mission to Scandinavia, it contains a report of the Norse paganism of the period.

Adam of Bremen was a guest at the court of Danish King Svend Estridsen, and even reported a visit to the Pagan temple in Uppsala, where he describes the Vikings in Uppsala as very hospitable but incredibly primitive. There are reasons to doubt if he visited Uppsala himself.

It would be fair to say that he wasn't a huge fan of Forn Siðr.

Annales Bertiniani, or the Annals of Saint Bertin, is a practical annual report of raids carried out by various Viking groups from Scandinavia in the Frankish areas, plundering Carolingian monasteries and episcopal cities 830-882. This is almost an accountant's spreadsheet.

Ahmad ibn Fadlan was a 10th-century envoy, famous for his account of his travels as a member of an embassy of the Abbasid caliphate to the king of the Volga Bulgars.

His account is most notable for providing a detailed description of the Rus Vikings, including eyewitness accounts of life as part of a trade caravan and witnessing a ship burial.

He describes the Vikings with a mix of fascination and horror.

Yacoub Al-Tartushi, a Jewish traveller, trader and diplomat from the Muslim Al-Andalus (present day Spain).

His travelogue, *Kitab al-Istibsar*, includes descriptions of various cities and regions as well as accounts of the customs and daily life of the people he encountered on his travels.

His work is widely known as providing the first description of the Vikings living in Heiðabýr, c.966.

He was *not* impressed!

He was particularly horrified – and used many negative superlatives about – their singing, that both men and women used *"artificial eye makeup"*, and (oh the horror!) that women had the right to divorce.

His original work is lost; only parts of it exist as (edited?) quotations in the works of other authors.

Unfortunately none of these works are decorated with accurate drawings, so we are relying on textual descriptions.

The different accounts give very conflicting descriptions of the Vikings, which is fair, since we are talking about groups of Vikings living very far from each other, subjected to very different influences.

It also makes sense since the writers have very different backgrounds.

The Anglo-Saxon chronicles claim that the Dane Vikings smelled fresh, bathed often, and were (unfairly) clean and vain, so they led Anglo-Saxon women astray. Even nobility.

Ahmad ibn Fadlan describes the Rus Vikings as *"the filthiest of all Allah's creatures"*.

Fadlan describes a female slave killed to be buried with her master. The Anglo-Saxon chronicles never mention anything like that (even if they would have loved to describe such a heathen wickedness!).

The Anglo-Saxon chronicles never mention tattoos, but Fadlan describes Vikings as being very tattooed, with floral patterns *"from their fingertips to the back of their necks"*.

MEDIEVAL WRITERS

As Iceland was a nation of expatriates the Icelanders were especially invested in keeping the history alive. For this reason a number of Icelandic authors created what is today known as The Icelandic Sagas.

This includes works like Egils saga Skalla-Grímssonar (Egil's Saga), Eiríks saga rauða (Saga of Erik the Red), Grænlendinga saga (Greenland saga), and 42 other sagas, written between 1200 and 1400, long after the Vikings had converted to Christianity, and in most cases 2-400 years after the events described had taken place.

The sagas are novel-like fictions based on historical figures and events. They focus on actions, events and themes such as murder, honour, families, eroticism, marriage and the relationship between the individual and society.

Before they were statically preserved on paper the sagas were retold in a more dynamic way by so-called skjalds, who would remember and recite the sagas in a poetic form.

Listening to a skjald reciting a saga was somewhat similar to going to a live concert now; you expect to recognise most of the lyrics and some of the tune, but you also expect the band to improvise and jam, giving you something extra and unexpected.

The sagas were not just intended for preserving and keeping the stories alive for future generations, but also for entertainment. Adding an invincible hero and a dragon to the story would obviously obscure the actual events a bit, but that was of secondary significance.

Even today it is common for writers to compose a fictional story with an actual historical background.

For historians to find a Dan Brown novel in a thousand years it will be equally confusing.

Question is: Do you want the truth, or do you want a good story?

The two most important mediaeval works are perhaps The Poetic Edda and the Prose Edda – also known as Snorri's Edda.

The Poetic Edda is, as the name suggests, poetry depicting religious myths and fables.

The poetry has been handed down in the oral tradition, and finally written down sometime between the years 800 and 1000, in western Norway and Iceland.

The Prose Edda is written by Snorri Sturluson, in Iceland, in 1220, and explains the Norse religion, as well as parts of the Poetic Edda, in prose.

This work is made for preserving and presenting knowledge and myths, rather than for artistic reasons.

Snorri was clearly very careful not to provoke his readers, as he was living in a Christian society, and might have been a devout Christian himself.

He has taken on the challenge of interpreting the Poetic Edda, and other stories, in such a way that people can grasp the storyline.

He even added some theories of his own, like the Æsir coming to Scandinavia from Troy, so it's hard for people nowadays to get the finer details about what common people in the Iron Age actually believed, and what stories they shared.

He has also sought to make a coherent story of all the fragments he had to begin with, which originated from a multitude of sources and traditions, so he had to make some editorial choices to succeed.

In one story Óðinn is married to Frigg, in another to Freyja, and in a third story Freyja and Freyr are two manifestations of the same person, while in the fourth they are married to respectively Odand and Gerd, and in the fifth to each other – Snorri had to clean up that mess, and set the story straight once and for all.

No matter how derailed Snorri got in his attempt to preserve, retell, interpret, and keep the Christian priests calm, all at the same time, it is the best keyhole we have to look through, into the Iron Age storytelling traditions.

We just have to read it with a huge grain of salt.

At the same time it is a hint about the trends in the early 1200s, where – for example – the whole world was fantasising about the destiny of the lost people of Troy, as Greek mythology was suddenly captivating everybody's imagination.

The Chronicle of the Danes (*"Gesta Danorum"*) is also from the 1200s, written by Saxo Grammaticus, in Denmark, commissioned by Bishop Absalon of Lund and King Valdemar the First.

It had to be dramatic and grand nationalistic propaganda.

From there we have the only mention of Lagerþa. We also have the story of prince Amleth, famously reinterpreted by William Shakespeare 400 years later (as Hamlet).

Saxo managed to create a direct bloodline from Ragnarr *"Loðbrók"* Sigurðsson to Knútr *"Ínn ríki"* Sveinsson, in effect making the present Danish royal family direct descendants of our boy Ragnarr.

One of the problems with the oral tradition is composite characters; more people becoming one person in the 1250th retell of the story.

A good example of this is Ragnarr Loðbrók. He rises to fame after slaying the invincible dragon-serpent, and dies in a pit of snakes.

There are several stories about him, and the only thing they have in common is the beginning, the end, and his name.

So he is a myth, a legend, and presumably a compound character.

We are pretty sure that Sigurðr *"Ormr í auga"* Áslaugsson, Halfdan *"Hvítserkr"*, Björn *"Járnsíða"*, and Ívarr *"hinn Beinlausi"* all were actual people, who claimed to be the sons of this legend, but not necessarily related to each other, in any way.

ARCHAEOLOGY

There is no shortage of finds from the Iron Age, and with modern technology it is possible to date things pretty accurately, and even take a small sample of the skeleton to say exactly where this person grew up, and where and how he or she lived as an adult.

We can analyse small pieces of wood with dendrochronology to see when, where, how and what.

With LIDAR and ground penetrating radar we can find graves, settlements, battlefields etc. pretty easily.

The law states that before any new building constructions can take place, the archaeologists are given time to excavate the site.

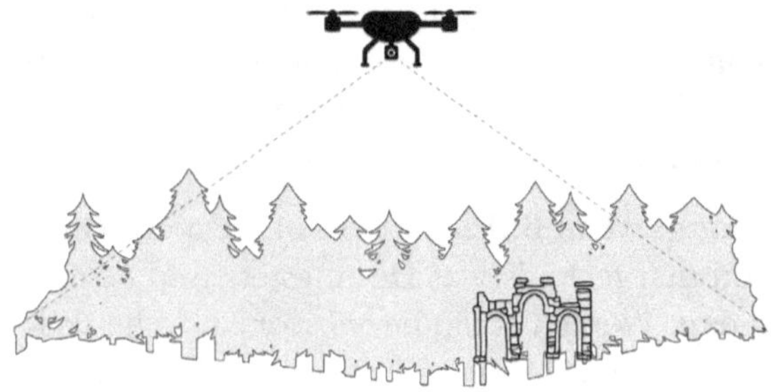

LIDAR

Ground penetrating radar

On top of all this a database is set up for amateurs with metal detectors to log their finds.

Modern day archaeologists are nothing short of spoiled brats!

Graves from the pre-Christian era are especially interesting, as Forn Siðr Vikings would be buried with grave goods for the afterlife.

Clothes, jewellery, household utensils, combs and ear cleaners, weapons, coins, food and even pets.

In a few cases, items from far Asia.

The problem is that these things do not come with an instruction manual (it took archaeologists a long time to figure out the purpose of the ear spoons), and some of the items might be gifts, not the deceased's belongings in life.

A famous warrior grave in Birka with lots of weapons contained a skeleton that recently was DNA tested, and turned out to be a woman. Women could be warriors, but the skeleton didn't have any signs of injuries of any kind. Could the weapons perhaps have belonged to her lost husband? Were they just tokens of importance? We don't know.

(In the time of writing this the lack of battle marks is actually disputed!)

Another important woman is found in the Oseberg ship burial in Norway. Judging from the grave goods she must have been one of the most influential people in Scandinavia, ever. She doesn't match with any sagas, chronicles, or runestones. We have simply no idea who she was.

In both Birka and Uppsala graves often contain Arab coins.

Many Rus Vikings served in the Varangian Guard in Constantinople, and came in possession of Arab coins in that context, but it doesn't mean the person in the grave had been in Baghdad himself. There was no reason to exchange currency as money was made of precious metals, and Vikings didn't mint coins themselves, so Dirhams were just money, and may have changed hands many times on the road from Baghdad to Birka.

Interpreting these findings always ends with a conflict between what is most *amazing* and what is most *likely*.

And interpretations will ever so often be influenced by present day trends.

When the label *"Viking Age"* was invented, in the 1870s, national pride was important, and Danish archaeologists got chills when they found something that was characteristically *Danish*.

Right now gender equality is trendy, and everybody's fantasising about finding an indisputable shield-maiden grave.

This constant conflict between the whims of the time and lack of actual facts doesn't make the interpretations easier.

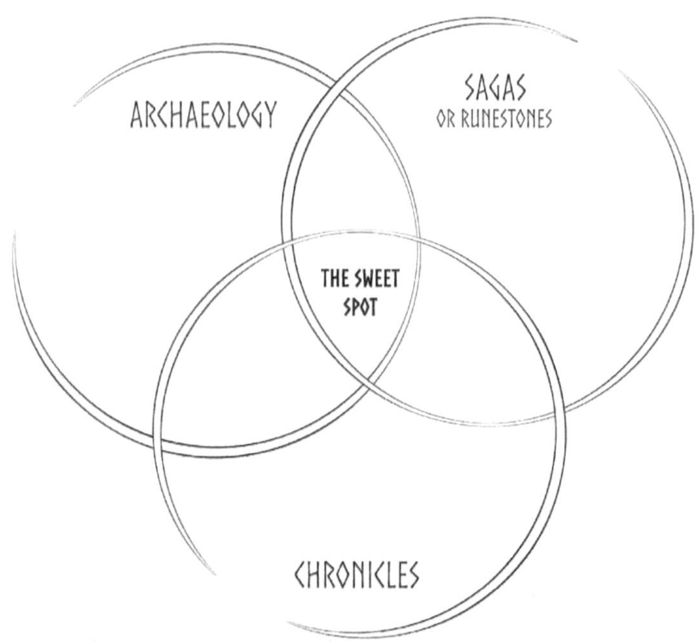

The closest thing we will get to confirmed history is when all inputs confirm each other, like the initial population of Iceland, Greenland and Vinland, right in the Sweet Spot. The Oseberg ship only in the Archaeology circle, or Haraldr Hárfagri only in the Saga circle, is rather frustrating.

BIO ARCHAEOLOGY

You might think of DNA as the most obvious way to trace the life history of a skeleton.

DNA can reveal your family history and place of origin to a certain degree.

Every child has two parents, and in 40 generations – a thousand years – it's 2^{40} = One trillion. As one trillion people didn't live on earth 1000 years ago, it's one trillion *positions*. These positions are filled with many of the same family over and over again; a large number of cousins and uncles x-times removed.

Basically your family tree doesn't resemble a tree, more like a diamond, pointed in both top and bottom, and with several overlapping lines crossing it.

You don't carry the DNA from all your ancestors in your backpack, however. Think of your mothers and fathers DNA as two decks of cards with 54 cards in each deck. When you were made, the stacks were mixed, and shuffled, for a new deck of 54 cards; maybe 28 from your mother, and 26 from your father. The remaining 54 cards are discarded. The same goes for your parents and your children. This is how you can have an ancestor with a hereditary disease, and no trace of it in your body. It also explains how inherited traces can be amplified if your family is practising serious inbreeding – 6 kings of hearts in the same deck…

Now it's possible to separate the male and female chromosomes in DNA, so scientists, who thought that the population of Iceland was mostly purebred descendants from Norway, basically inbreeding for several generations, found that it turned out to be blokes from Norway who made a small detour to Ireland and picked up some Cailins, before settling on Iceland.

But DNA can't tell us if the Irish lasses were *culturally* Danes, and made hearts around the name Haraldr in their diaries, or so Irish they were kidnapped and taken to Iceland kicking and screaming.

You can't test if you have Viking DNA, only if your DNA matches the present population in Scandinavia. But Viking

DNA will contain traces of Anglo-Saxons, Sámi, Frisians, Slavic tribes, and maybe an exotic babe from Miklagarðr, as Vikings have shared and collected DNA in a radius of about 3000 kilometres.

White supremacist fuckheads – sorry: *"Nordicists"* – in the USA thought they could use DNA to prove Viking descent, expecting a lot of Gustaf Vasa in their veins. When the results came back they decided DNA science is an evil Jewish conspiracy hoax.

But there's more to Bio Archaeology than DNA.

You are what you eat, and everything you eat and drink will be logged in your body. The calcium in yesterday's breakfast bacon will be tomorrow's replacement cells in your skeleton.

Especially the isotopic ratio variations of strontium and oxygen will incorporate quite specific geographic signatures in your body.

"I was in Spain for a couple of weeks; it has become a part of my body". Yes, it literally has!

If we make a cross section of a sample of your skeleton, slices will reveal where you have lived your entire life: Birka 15 years, Holmgarðr 2 years, Kiev 6 months, Miklagarðr 5 years, Kiev 3 years, Ribe 3 years, Jórik 2 years…

Teeth will confirm where you grew up, and the fastest growing part of your body – your hair – will add a very specific travel log of the last year, or so: Jórik 3 months, London 1 month, Jórik 2 months, Repton 1 week.

Skeletons, teeth and hair will in many cases last for thousands of years if buried in good soil.

Oh, I will be *so* blood eagled because of this simplification… Fair enough.

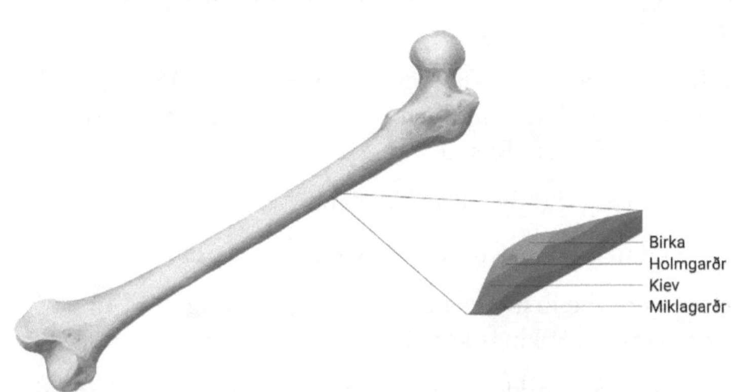

WHAT DON'T WE KNOW?

The list of unanswered questions is practically endless, but some of the questions we would really like the answers to include:

How did they conduct religious rituals, like prayers, offerings, weddings, knee-setting (the initiation of a new-born child), funerals, etc.?
There must have been huge differences over time, and from one place to the next, so this is actually thousands of answers we are looking for.

What was the actual, specific, relations between men and women, children and adults, slaves and owners, citizens and chieftains? Civil rights? Fair trials? Financial disputes? Polygamy? Infidelity? Homosexuality? How was all this handled?
Again, there must have been huge differences…

Were they as reserved one moment, and unrestrained the next, as present day Scandinavians? Equally blasphemous?

Equally jovial? How far back can we trace these personality traits?

What was the day-to-day relation between the Vikings and the local population in the countries where they settled (England, France, Russia, etc.)?

Why, exactly, did they leave Vinland?

When and why, exactly, did they leave Greenland?

How were the first encounters between Vikings and Inuits? And between Vikings and native Canadians?

How was the workload distributed between men and women?
It would be funny – and very modern – if all our guesses are complete wrong.

How many women participated in raids?

Were explorations, long distance voyages, trading and raiding just as common in the Bronze Age as in the Iron Age (as a growing number of archaeologists suggests)?

Language; how easy or difficult was it for Anglo-Saxons, Danes and Rus to communicate?

Did the Vikings write stories and accounts on perishable materials that have now dissolved? It must be difficult to run a business without bookkeeping.
(Bookkeeping on clay tablets is the reason why we know so much more about much older civilisations in the Middle East.)

How far did they travel east?

Items from India might have changed hands hundreds of times en route to Scandinavia, but could have been in the same pocket all the way (unlikely, but…)

What will be the next completely mind-blowing archaeological find?

Ever so often we believe that a specific Viking expedition *"discovered"* something new, like the Shetland Islands, the mouth of the Dnieper river, or the entry to the Mediterranean sea, only to discover next that they already knew, and they were definitely not *"venturing into the unknown"*.

Landing by the Lindisfarne monastery was not *"a stroke of luck"*, and Leifur Eiríksson didn't *"discover"* Vinland. They were following a detailed plan.

So our important historical and archaeological discoveries are almost never about *"what happened next"*, but about *"what happened before"*.

It's very hip and modern: We are writing prequels.

WHAT'S SO COOL ABOUT THE VIKING SHIPS?

To sail the oceans without capsizing a ship needs a deep keel, that in turn will prevent the ship from going into shallow water.

So traditionally you would have to find a harbour with deep water.

Alternatively anchoring a distance from land, and transferring crew and cargo to smaller boats, to go to shore.

In order to venture into rivers or canals you would have to change boat to a flat-bottomed vessel.

It was still worth the effort since travelling on water would give you much more speed and cargo hold than horse or cattle carriages.

The Vikings designed a boat that was basically flat-bottomed, except for a long and shallow keel, and the perfect height/length/width ratio not to capsize on ocean voyages, and the possibility to go all the way up to the beach, into the rivers and canals, and so light weight that it was possible to carry the ships over land. The last thing was practical on the Dnieper river, where numerous waterfalls make sailing impossible, and places, where rivers aren't connected to a nearby lake you want to cross.

Obviously it also gave them the opportunity to attack a village or monastery that was close to water, but inaccessible to traditional larger boats, due to the shallow waters.

Furthermore they were clinker built, which is the overlapping of planks riveted together, which made the hull slightly flexible in the waves, so the ship would almost cut through the waves, and not break apart when being exposed to shock, like hard waves, hard wind, cliffs or sandy beaches.

They could cross the ocean from Denmark to England, go up the river, ground the boat on a small beach, raid a monastery, and be back in the ocean, heading back to Denmark so fast, the locals thought it was supernatural.

I recently heard a historian comparing it to a drive-by-shooting…

Today, two thousand years later, huge container ships are built with the same proportionality, and with a keel that is basically a long cylinder spanning the entire length of the ship.

It is worth noticing that even though Denmark is now a micronation, many of the largest container vessels in the sea are owned by the Danish Mærsk Line.

Obviously the huge sail made travel faster and easier, and made the Vikings travel much further than they did before the sail was introduced.

Weaving the sail was extremely time consuming, and a sail was almost as expensive as the ship itself – adding to the gender equality, as sails would presumably most oftenly be made by women.

The design of the sail and mast was not as good as the triangular sails known in the Mediterranean and the red sea, however, as the angle could only be altered so many degrees, and *"tacking"* against the wind would bring the ship far off course, both starboard and backboard directions, as you zig-zag to use the wind in your favour.

Another design flaw, seen with modern eyes, is the small rudder, placed in the back on the starboard side (hence the name: Starboard literally means steering side). This gave limited manoeuvrability, and the roars would come into action to make a sharp turn.

The larger boats, created for long voyages, were large enough to carry crew, cargo, supplies and even livestock – and bring back loot and slaves.

To save space on board hooks on the railing could hold the large shields on the outside of the ship. That is one easily recognizable design feature, so iconic a Viking ship will always be depicted with the shields, even if it might have only been a small minority of the boats that had that feature. We don't know.

Another recognisable feature is the tail in the back and the head in the front depicting a dragon, actually giving the Viking ships the nickname Dragon Ships.

Keep in mind that a dragon in the Viking mythology was not fire spewing and winged, but in fact a large snake, or serpent, and just one of many translations of the old Norse word *"ormr"*.

(See the Viking Encyclopedia elsewhere in this book.)

The best preserved ships from the Iron Age are the Oseberg ship discovered in a large burial mound at the Oseberg farm near Tønsberg in Norway, and the Gokstad ship, a 9th-century Viking ship found in a burial mound at Gokstad in Sandar, Sandefjord, Vestfold, Norway. Both are displayed at the Viking Ship Museum in Oslo.

In Roskilde fjord, in Denmark, five ships were sunk on purpose, presumably in order to prevent enemy attacks. These ships (The Skuldelev Ships) were found in 1962 and are now on display in Roskilde Viking Ship Museum.

This museum has an ongoing production of replicas, some of them built using Iron Age tools, and it is possible to go on tour with them.

But others are making Viking ships as well: In 2012 Draken Harald Hårfagre was launched and the trial sailing began. The summer of 2014 Draken Harald Hårfagre made her first ocean going voyage, from Haugesund, Norway, to Liverpool, England and back again.

In late April 2016 Draken Harald Hårfagre left her home port in Haugesund, Norway and sailed off for a challenging voyage across the North Atlantic Ocean, to Lerwick, Torshavn, Reykjavik, Qaqortoq, Quebec, Montreal, Toronto, Chicago and New York.

Bjørn Heyerdahl, grandson to Kon-Tiki-famous Thor Heyerdahl, has built a Viking ship with the intent to sail from Oslo to Miklagarðr on the *Midgard Expedition; "The search for intelligent life on earth".*

We have absolutely no bloody idea when the design of these ships came about, as every archaeological excavation takes us further back in time.

2,700 year old petroglyphs (rock carvings) in Sweden suggest they were on to *something* already in the Bronze Age.

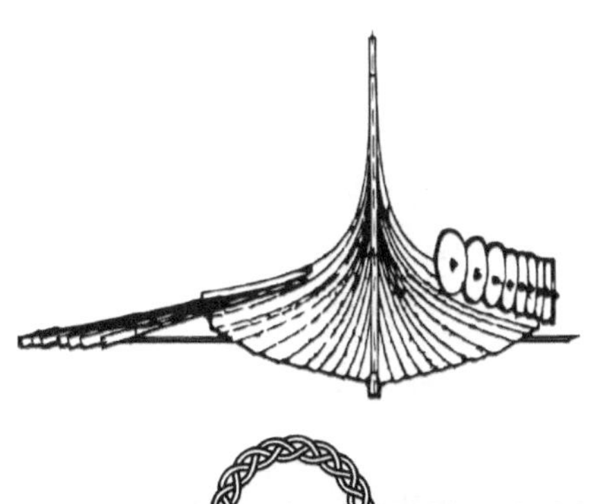

HOW DID THE IRON AGE VIKINGS LIVE?

Most lived in rather small wooden houses with steep roofs. In the centre of the house there would be a stone set open fireplace with an iron frame above, to hang a metal pot for cooking.

In one end of the house, on all three sides, short beds would be built up to the outer wall, lined with sheep skins. They slept more or less sitting up.

Instead of an opening in the roof directly above the fireplace, like most others made at that time, the Vikings would have the opening in each end of the house, at the top of the gable.

The chieftains house was the largest, *"the long hall"*, with plenty of room for guests and feasts, religious rites, meetings and all kinds of social gatherings, including a welcome ceremony for everyone who arrived in the village.
And absolutely no privacy, if he actually lived there.

In the long hall, and other larger buildings, the walls would curve slightly, almost like a ship, to make the construction more resilient.

None of the houses – not even the long hall – would have windows until around year 800. The climate in Scandinavia doesn't allow windows without thick glass, which wasn't available.

The fireplace in the centre of the long hall would be approximately one metre wide and three to four metres long.

Houses would often be decorated inside with intricate wood carving and woven tapestries.

Outside the roof rafters could be extended at the ends and carved like dragon heads.

Parts of the houses could be painted in dark red, blue, green or yellow colours. Usually only corner posts, the gable and the door.

In some areas people would treat the wood by carefully burning the surface, to make it resistant to rot and mould.

Farms would be medium size houses, still one big room, with a fireplace in the centre.

The family would sleep in one end of the house, while the thralls (slaves) would sleep in the other end, in winter time, along with the livestock.

The precious – and expensive – part of the house was the supporting columns or pillars; high quality timber with beautiful carvings. When a family moved they would tear down the house, but take the pillars with them.

It is actually told that when Eiríkur *"Rauði"* Þorvaldsson was exiled from Iceland he asked a friend to take care of his columns, and when he failed to do so Eiríkur killed him, on return.

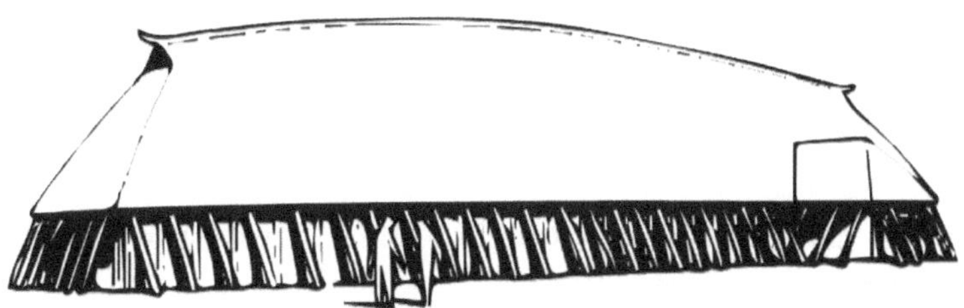

WHAT DID THE VIKINGS EAT?

Cabbage, beets, oats, barley, rye and wheat, chicken, pork, lamb and – rarely – beef.

Most servings would be porridge, but occasionally bread would be served as well.

Bread was especially practical to bring along on travels. Meat would be roasted at the fireplace.

Generally speaking the diet was rather healthy, and even if meat wasn't served every day, the Vikings would eat more meat than most other people in the world, a thousand years ago. This is one of the reasons for Scandinavians to be a few centimetres longer than other Europeans, on average, and slightly more resistant to many illnesses.

Obviously many Vikings were increasingly inspired by their new neighbours in England, Kievan Rus and Normandy, and the diets became more varied when we close in on the ninth century.

Food preparation and processing was primarily done for preservation, as most crops are harvested in the autumn, so the supply is plentiful and relatively fresh during the winter months, but as spring approaches it would become problematic, and during the first months of summer starvation would set in.

To counter this, berries would be boiled in honey and sealed, and fish and meat would be dried, smoked or salted, and so on.

While the Viking's diet was rather healthy for the time, I will not recommend that you replicate it, since you are presumably not working 12 hours in the fields, without mechanical tools. They would probably need 8-10 times as many carbo-hydrates as you do, and 5-6 times as much fat.

This is said casually with the caveat that I am not a dietitian.

WHAT DID THE VIKINGS DRINK?

Water, milk, beer, wine and mead.

It's popular in movies to depict Vikings drinking mead from a large cow's horn.

I would love to serve a pint of mead for any Viking fan, and see the reaction. Mead is a rather thick and sweet drink, and resembles dessert wines, like port or sherry. Not exactly something you drink in large quantities, and no doubt considered a luxury.

No, the horns would most likely be filled with beer.

The beer was spontaneously fermented, presumably slightly bitter with citrus notes, and quite watered down, as people would drink it in rather large quantities.

Ribe Bryghus, in Denmark, actually made a beer in 2010 based on finds in an archaeological excavation.

Wine was imported from central and southern Europe.

WHAT LANGUAGE DID THE VIKINGS SPEAK?

The Vikings spoke old Norse, obviously with many different dialects.

Since the Viking Age the language has evolved into Danish, Norwegian, Swedish and Icelandic, where the last is least influenced by other languages, and therefore closest to the Viking's language. That doesn't mean Iceland people would be able to understand a Viking from 790 without problems.

The three other languages have been heavily influenced by French and German, and now by modern English.

But the Vikings language has also had a serious impact on English and other languages, and it's interesting to know that thousands of words in modern English originate in old Norse: Egg, knife, wife, window, sky, son, daughter, church, etc.

HOW DID THE VIKINGS WRITE?

Elder fuþark (c. 0 - 800 AD)

Younger fuþark (c. 700 - 1400 AD)

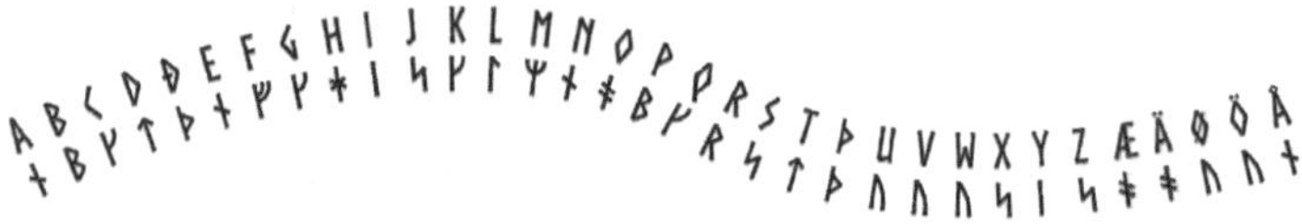

Anglo-Saxon fuþark (c. 400 - 1300 AD)

Not all letters existed in the rune alphabet so some letters might share a rune.

":" is:used:for:separating:words.

To translate write phonetically: Michael = Mikal

At www.vikingr.site you can find a latin to fuþark translator.

Danish and Norwegian alphabet (c. 900 AD – present day)
ABCDEFGHIJKLMNOPQRSTUVWXYZÆØÅ
abcdefghijklmnopqrstuvwxyzæøå

Swedish alphabet (c. 900 AD – present day)
ABCDEFGHIJKLMNOPQRSTUVWXYZÅÄÖ
abcdefghijklmnopqrstuvwxyzåäö

Icelandic alphabet (c. 900 AD – present day)

AÁBDÐEÉFGHIÍJKLMNOÓPRSTUÚVXYÝÞÆÖ
aábdðeéfghiíjklmnoóprstuúvxyýþæø

Note that there are huge overlaps in use, and all have under-gone changes over the years.

[U36]

WHAT ARE RUNESTONES AND RUNESTICKS?

[DR42]

A runestone is typically a two metre tall stone with a more-or-less flat surface, engraved with runes and decorations.

You might think that runestones are a give-away to historians.

But...

There were no schools, no examinations, no dictionaries, and people would spell as they saw fit, adding to the local variations.

Often they would write in a made up shorthand, similar to modern day text messages, like *"C U L8"* (*"See you later"*).

This makes reading rune stones exceptionally difficult, and scholars argue a lot about the contents.

Some people believe that specific runes were allocated to specific Æsir, like the T rune allocated to Týr. That, however, is not an established rule, but rather a result of this short-hand writing. In modern days *"ROFL"* means *"Rolling on the floor laughing"*, but it doesn't mean that *"L"* always means *"Laughing"*.

The same way *"T"* doesn't mean *"Týr"* completely out of context. It presumably does, when engraved on a weapon or shield, but not on a doorpost to a farm.

The rune stones are unevenly distributed in Scandinavia: Denmark has 250 rune stones, Norway has 50 while Iceland has none. Sweden has more than 2,500.

Outside of Scandinavia, the Isle of Man stands out with its 30 rune stones from the 9th century and early 11th century.

Scattered rune stones have also been found in England, Ireland, Scotland and the Faroe Islands.

Sometimes the text would be pure self promotion: *"Eskill Skulkason had this stone raised to himself. Ever will stand this memorial that Eskill made."* [Dr 212].

The text is most oftenly a commemoration of a fallen warrior, but even a praise to the creators of the stone:

"Hvatarr and Heilgeirr raised the stone in memory of Helgi, their father. He travelled to the west with the Vikingr." [G370].

The most detailed and famous rune stones is the pair standing in Jelling, Denmark, where the largest of the two states:

"Haraldr konungr bað gorva kumbl þausi aft Gorm faður sinn auk aft Þórví móður sína. Sá Haraldr es sér vann Danmark alla auk Norveg auk dani gærði kristna."

In English: *"King Haraldr ordered this monument made in memory of Gormr, his father, and in memory of Thyrvé, his mother; that Haraldr who won for himself all of Denmark and Norway and made the Danes Christian."* [DR42].

What is remarkable about the stone is that even if it proclaimed Denmark to be Christian, and is therefore referred to as the *"Birth Certificate of Denmark"*, making it the most famous runestone in the world, the propaganda is slightly sketchy: The man portrayed on the stone has his arms spread out, like the crucified Jesus, but resembles a long tradition of depicting Óðinn, entangled in a tree with a pointy beard. Is it a morph between the two? Was he playing both horses?

One thing's for certain: All Danes reading this will open their passport, look at the first page, where the runestone is printed, and think *"What the f…???"*.

Trends have changed a lot over the years, and if I had made a headstone for my late brother stating *"The mighty writer Hassan made this stone in honour of my cool brother Lars"*. I am confident most people would find it to be rather bad taste (so I didn't).

All rune stones can be found in www.runesdb.eu with references like [DR41].

In Riksantikvarieämbetet in Stockholm Laila Kitzler Åhfeldt has developed a method to identify stonemasons of runestones by scanning the runestones, and basically use the same kind of software as you would use to recognise fingerprints. Every mason has his own rhythm and style in his muscle memory, and the runes engraved reveal this. That is how we know that Ravnunge Tue who made both Jelling stones also made the Læborg stone [SJy37] and a few more.

Rune sticks are small pieces of wood with short poetry, and sometimes messages to be sent. A Viking Age SMS. Until recently they have been quite a rarity, but presently a larger quantity is being found in southern Norway.

U283

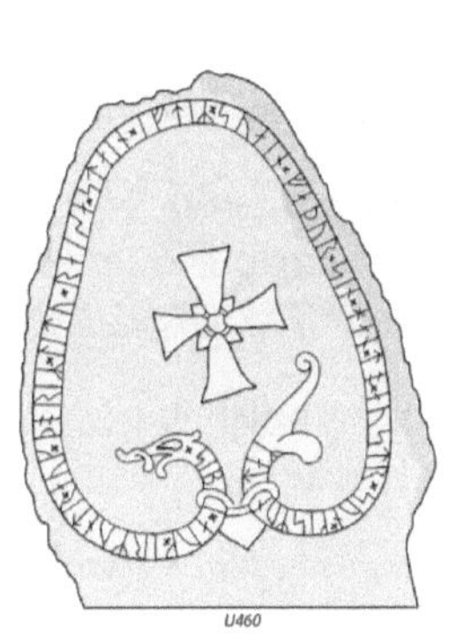
U460

DR42

WHAT ARE VIKING NAMES LIKE?

First names were most oftenly Æsir, animals, places or events.

Boys could be named things like Björn (Bear), Ulf (Wolf), Haraldr (Warlord) Þórr or even Viking.

Girls could be named Helga (Holy) or Astrið (Beautiful God), etc.

Viking names are still given to approximately half of all children in Scandinavia.

Surnames would be patronymic; the father's name plus *"son"*, if it was indeed a son, or *"dottír"* if it was a daughter.

In a few instances it could be the mother's name plus *"son"*/*"dottír"*, like the famous Danish King Svend Estridsson – the son of Queen Estrid.

This practice ended about 150 years ago in Scandinavia, but is still in use in Iceland, where Halgrim's daughter will have the surname Halgrimsdottir.

Many were given a nickname, in life or afterwards.

Things like *"Victory"*, *"The Great"* and *"The Bald"* are pedestrian, but there are a few curious ones in the sagas, like *"Boneless"*, *"Another Day"* and *"The Misguided"*.

It was necessary since a ridiculously large number of men were called Valdemar or Haraldr.

(*"Will the real Haraldr Valdemarson please stand up?"*)

Viking names that are still popular today includes (spelling may vary):

GIRLS NAMES	BOYS NAMES
Astrid	Arne
Bodil	Bjørn
Freja	Bo
Frida	Erik
Gro	Frode
Gudrun	Gorm
Gunhild	Gunnar
Helga	Harald
Hilda	Ivar
Inga	Knud
Ingrid	Leif
Liv	Magnus
Ragnhild	Ragnar
Randi	Rune
Saga	Sten
Sif	Sune
Sigrid	Svend
Solveig	Thor
Thyra	Toke
Tove	Troels
Åse	Ulf

DID THE VIKINGS REALLY NAME EVERYTHING?

Not everything, but important unique belongings, like the sword, axe and ship were named.

Today it would be your car, laptop and dishwasher.

It makes things more relatable and gives you a sense of pride and gratitude in objects.

Minor quirks are somewhat more acceptable...

My smartphone is named Halgrim, my bicycle is named Sleipner, and I have a small palm tree named Oluf, and it does add some personality to my stuff.

Naming things – especially ships – is not a Viking invention, however, as the ancient mariners of Greece, Egypt and Rome also held naming rites when launching their new vessels, as a way of asking their gods to protect their ships.

WHAT DID THE IRON AGE VIKINGS LOOK LIKE?

The men would most oftenly wear a tunic and trousers.

Women would often wear a simple dress with an apron on top, not just for protection, but as a fashion statement.

These basics were most oftenly made of wool or hemp.

A cape would be used in the winter months, made of wool or fur.

The Rus Vikings adopted the liking for bright colours in the east, while the Danes didn't get that kind of inspiration in the west.

Thousands of Viking graves have been opened, and we have found an abundance of bones, hair, and jewellery, but no skin is preserved, so we have absolutely no idea about their makeup or tattoos.

Accurate drawing wasn't a thing, a thousand years ago, so we must rely on contemporary written sources.

According to Arabic sources the Rus Vikings were heavily tattooed, with floral patterns.

If this custom was brought from home, in present day Sweden, or picked up in contact with Slavic tribes, we don't know.

The Danes, described intensely by English and Frankish monks, are never mentioned to have been tattooed at all.

What we know with certainty, however, is that both men and women, in both east and west, had a strong fixation on braided hair and beard.

It couldn't be advanced enough. Though Óðinn is most oftenly the head Æsir, most people would wear Mjölnír (Þórr's hammer) in a necklace, since Þórr is the main protector of humans. From around 950 to 1300 more and more people would wear a Christian cross, or a morph between the two.

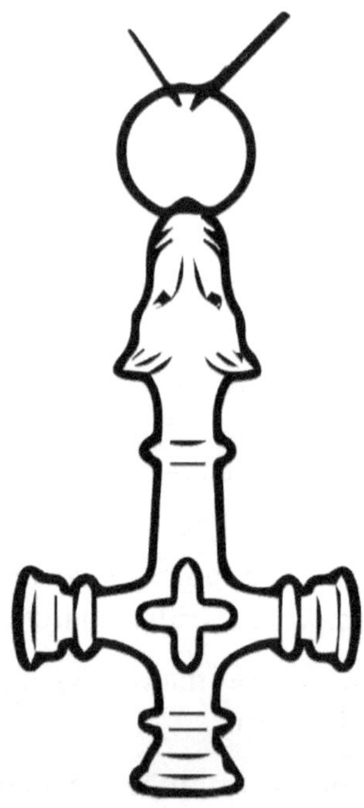

The Wolf Cross is found in Iceland, and appears to be a morph between a Mjölnír, a cross and a wolf. As there are several wolves mentioned in the sagas it's impossible to guess which one, and why it is depicted.

(No. Absolutely not! An upside-down cross is not "satanic". That idea didn't exist until c.1980. An upside-down cross is either just a cross, or specifically the cross of Saint Peter, who was viciously crucified upside-down in Rome, according to Christian mythology.)

AREN'T ALL IRON AGE VIKINGS BLOND?

I'm on a bit of a slippery slope here, as science is very vague, and it's a sensible subject, for some reason, so I'll give you a simple answer, with all kinds of reservations.

In the beginning of the Iron Age most Vikings were dark haired, like the majority of the world's population. By selectively taking slaves in the Slavic areas – what would become Kievan Rus – they brought home people with genetics for blond hair, and had children with some of them. The blond became coveted and by sexual selection more and more people became blond, as the Viking Age progressed.

The trend continues, and scientists believe there are a much higher percentage of blond people in Scandinavia today than in the Iron Age.
(Add to them the number of peroxide blondes!)

The blond slaves were also popular in the Byzantine Empire, and today there's a disproportionately high percentage of blond people in present day western Turkey.

At the risk of stepping into a thorn bush I'll say the gene for blond hair originates in northern Asia (Siberia), and came to Scandinavia from the general vicinity of present day Ukraine.

The habit of raping and/or marrying slaves is a Viking thing...

Light skin is not just a question of ethnicity, but develops in areas where the population needs it to better absorb vitamin D. Many (north-) Asians are just as pale as Scandinavians.

WERE THE VIKINGS DIRTY OR CLEAN?

Yes. How do you like that for an answer?

Compared to most people living today they would probably benefit from a shower and a toothbrush.

Compared to Anglo-Saxons they were extremely clean.

As mentioned, they had developed an appreciation for cleanliness, without the knowledge about all the microscopic reasons to keep clean, and English letter- and chronicle writers actually complain that Saxon women preferred the Viking men because of their cleanliness, vanity and fresh scent.

John of Wallingford writes: *"The Danes made themselves too acceptable to English women by their elegant manners and their care of their person. They combed their hair every day, bathed every Saturday, and even changed their garments often. They set off their persons by many such frivolous devices. In this manner, they laid siege to the virtue of the married women and persuaded the daughters, even of the nobles, to be their concubines."*

Vikings didn't just own a nail cleaner and an ear cleaner (*"ear spoon"*), but showed them off, often made of bone or precious metal, hanging from the belt for all to see, and always buried with them and a comb.

The hair and beard were braided to keep dirt and vermin out.

The benefits of cleanliness were more than just vanity and more sex, but people lived longer, with better health, lower child mortality, and better chances of surviving wounds.

It's worth remembering that many warriors, who didn't die on the battlefield, died a few days later from infected wounds, so washing the wounds made a huge difference.

So, yes, the Vikings were very clean and healthy.

But compared to the Muslims in Al-Andalus and the Abbasid caliphate they were dirty.

Islam dictates how you should wash before prayer – several times a day – before and after meals, and before and after having sex.

The Vikings didn't exactly live up to that standard, and Ahmad ibn Fadlan, who met the Rus Vikings somewhere near the Caspian sea in 921, writes:

"They are the filthiest of all Allah's creatures: They do not purify themselves after excreting or urinating or wash themselves when in a state of ritual impurity after coitus and do not even wash their hands after food."

He goes on to describe that a servant (slave?) brings a water bowl for a group of men, and they all wash their hands, face, and blow their nose in the same water.
He is disgusted, to put it mildly.

Now it is too obvious for me to emphasise that both Saxon and Arab writers have reasons to exaggerate, in order to fit their narrative, but it's probably safe to say the Viking's level of cleanliness fit somewhere in between English and Muslim standards.

It is also worth mentioning that the Christian priests spread the message that bathing would lead to pneumonia and many north Europeans would not take a single bath in their entire lifetime, for that reason. In that context it's easy to stand out as fresh and clean.

The Vikings general health seems to have suffered a bit from the conversion to Christianity, but there may be other reasons why life expectancy was shortened in the early Middle Ages.

WHAT WEAPONS DID THE VIKINGS USE?

Swords have been found in rich people's graves, but they were the weapons for the higher ranks in society. Most would use the tools already available in the farm: The axe.

Before getting into trouble many would change the handle from the normal c. 50 cm. to a much longer handle, about 100 cm.

The rich would obviously have two different types of axes; one for wood work and an assault axe.

Spears and knives were used as well, and to add range they would use bow and arrow.

What separates the Vikings from many other warriors was the way they would use the shield, not only for protection, but actually as a weapon.

Both contemporary Frankish and Byzantine sources mention this, so it was a technique known by both Danes and Rus.

The shield wall was not a Viking invention, and not unique to the Vikings, and was known by the Roman Empire, and presumably even earlier.

As they encountered foreign weapons they would quickly adopt these into their armoury, including *"Greek Fire"*, which is thick sticky flammable liquids on the battlefield, or thrown on the enemies, and set alight. It's basically a thousands of years old edition of napalm.

Oddly enough two kinds of weapons are still not found in Viking graves: The crossbow and the English longbow.

The Vikings were frontrunners in the development of high quality steel, and actually made fortunes on weapons export.

WHAT DID THE IRON AGE VIKINGS EXPORT?

As mentioned they exported high quality steel weapons, but also a long range of other products that were unique to Scandinavia, like certain kinds of fur or skin, amber, whale oil, ivory from narwhals and walrus, and lots and lots of slaves, from Scandinavia, Ireland, England, Scotland and the Slavic areas in and around Kievan Rus.

To be a hotshot in the Byzantine realm you would need to trade with the Rus to get your hands on a blond slave, amber and white fur.

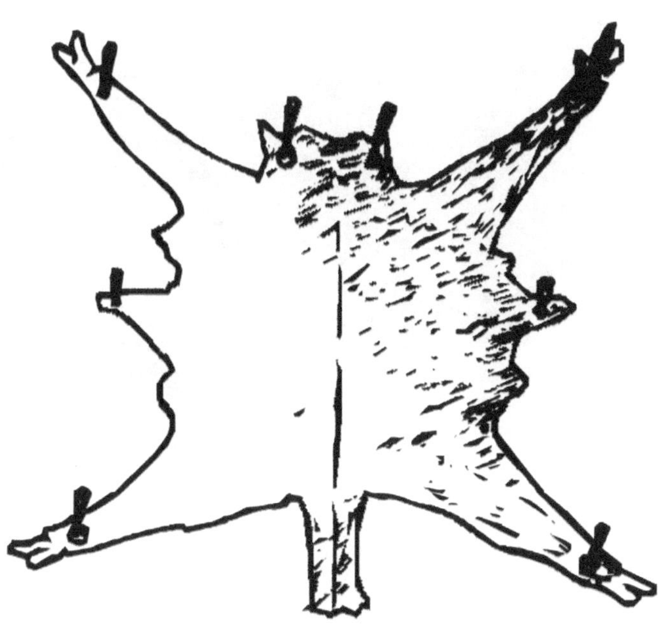

WHAT DID THE IRON AGE VIKINGS IMPORT?

Coins, silk and other fine fabrics, precious stones, precious metals, wine, chemicals to dye fabric, precision tools of any kind, and exotic handicrafts like drinking glasses, jewellery, and advanced pottery.

To show off riches in Scandinavia you needed a blue shirt and a huge gold necklace with precious stones, and a glass of red wine in your hand.

WHAT DID THE IRON AGE VIKINGS STEAL?

Precious metal objects, precious stones, all sorts of jewellery, valuable church inventory and accessories, fine clothes and other small objects, money, and most of all people – enslaving people, and stealing people who were already slaves.

WAS THERE EVER A BIG VIKING EMPIRE?

For a very short period there was actually a very big Viking Kingdom in the west. A small part of northern Germany, a substantial part of England, a tiny piece of Poland, all of Denmark, southernmost part of Sweden, and two thirds of Norway was one kingdom, under King Knútr *"Ínn ríki"* Sveinsson (Cnut *"the Great"*).

At the same time other Vikings ruled Ireland, Iceland and Greenland independently.

Up until then the Viking controlled areas in the west consisted of several minor kingdoms, constantly changing alliances and getting into new disputes.

In the east the situation was more stable, where Rus Vikings ruled from central Sweden, through the Baltic states, western Russia, Belarus and Ukraine, parts of Hungary and Bulgaria, to a part of European Turkey – all the way from Birka to Miklagarðr – for several hundred years.

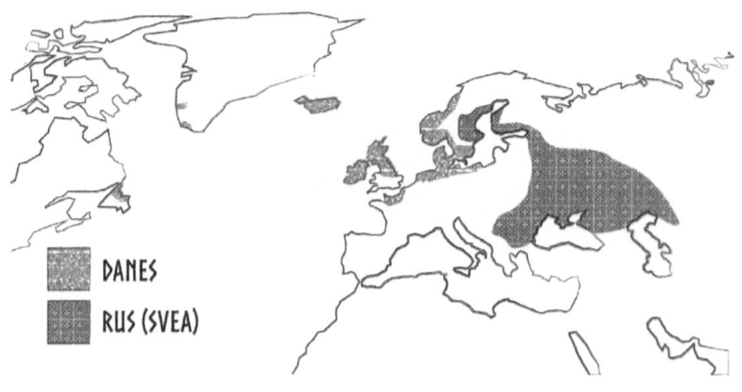

WHERE WERE THE MOST IMPORTANT IRON AGE VIKING CITIES?

A few important cities were founded by the Vikings, but most were occupied and expanded during the Iron Age.

Among the most important were Ribe, Dublin, Jórvik (York), Holmgarðr (Novgorod), Kyiv, Jelling, Roskilde, Uppsala, Uppåkra, Birka, Sigtuna and Heiðabýr.

Birka doesn't exist anymore, but was situated only a few kilometres from present day Stockholm, so it's more likely moved than eradicated.

Heiðabýr was raided and burned in 1049.

Other cities have been important for a short while, and others have grown to importance after the Iron Age.

You might say London had been important since the Roman Empire, and still is today, but even though the Vikings fought hard for it, it wasn't actually very important in the Viking Age. Decisions were made in Jórvik, and it was in Jórvik the money was made.

Miklagarðr was never occupied by Vikings, but hugely important to them. Miklagarðr literally means *"The Big City"*.

WHAT'S THE RELATION BETWEEN VIKINGS, FRISIANS, SÁMI, ANGLO-SAXONS, ETC.?

I'll keep the puzzle as simple as possible – and it will still be complicated!

When the ice cape disappeared from Scandinavia 12,000 years ago some of the first inhabitants came from the east, and became the Sámi people, who lived – and still live – in the northernmost part of the Scandinavian peninsula, herding reindeer in a semi-nomadic lifestyle.

They have an ethnicity and a language of their own, that is not related to old Norse.

The environment they live in is of little interest to hunter-gatherers and farmers, so there has been very limited contact between them and most other groups in Scandinavia, until the late middle age.

In southern Finland the Finns arrived from the area around the Ural mountains, in present day Russia.

The Sámi and the Finns apparently got along so well that their languages became very closely knit.

South of Scandinavia, in an area that is present day northern France, Germany and the Netherlands, were the Germanic tribes. One of the few groups of people in Europe that the Roman Empire never managed to conquer.

The Germanic had two offsprings: The Norse, in present day southern Sweden, and the Saxons in present day north-western Germany and Jutland (in Denmark).

As the Roman Empire collapsed around 500 AD people started moving around in large groups, known as the Migration period.

The Norse were divided into two groups, the Rus and the Danes (keeping it simple…).

The Danes took up the southern part of Scandinavia; Denmark, southern Sweden and Norway, and pushed the Saxons out of Denmark.

The Rus moved through, or around, present day Småland, to inhabit the area around Lake Mälaren in central Sweden.

The Saxons flooded into present day England, which was, by then, inhabited by the Romano-British people, and together they became the Anglo-Saxons.

In northern Scotland you would find the Picts, and in Ireland the Irish.

The Irish invaded the Picts territory, and the outcome was the Scots.

The Germanic tribes gave birth to two more offsprings: The Frisians and the Frankish.

For a time around the early 7th century there seems to have been some kind of competition between the Frisian and the Danes about the dominance of the sea in their general vicinity.

We don't hear a lot about the Frisians after that… (A little unfair, but bear with me.)

As mentioned there was an unbroken link between the Danes and the Rus, when it comes to trade and language, though DNA reveals there has been very little interbreeding.

So by 700 AD we have a few separated groups of people, with the Sámi and Finns keeping to themselves in northern and easternmost Scandinavia, the Rus and Danes occupying all of southern and central Scandinavia, The Anglo-Saxons in England, the Scots in Scotland, the Irish in Ireland, and the Frankish south of Scandinavia.

The groups consisted of several – if not hundreds – of small kingdoms, but they had most of their religious convictions in common, and traded with each other, as well as raided and enslaved each other. I mean all of them.

In western Norway there has been trading going on even between the Danes and the Sámi, as archaeological findings reveal, and the sagas tell of king Haraldr Hárfagri marrying the Sámi princess Snøfrid Svåsedottir, but other than that there has been almost no contact.

The Anglo-Saxons had become Christian, and even if the many English kingdoms were at constant war with each other, no one would dare attack a church or monastery, which left them rather unprotected. A niche for people who didn't give a shit.

For the first couple of hundred years of the Iron Age the different groups of Danes didn't cooperate, but traded and raided independently, with or against each other and the English, with constantly changing alliances.

It was a mess.

The result of this mess was more and more resilient alliances, and growing kingdoms.

In the south Charlemagne (or Charles the Great) created the Holy Roman Empire, that stretched from central Italy to the

Danish border, and from eastern France into the middle of Poland (speaking in present day countries).

The English kingdoms of Mercia, Wessex, Northumbria, East Anglia, etc. experimented with different kinds of alliances.

This development led to the Danes coming together, and forming their own alliances, and the infamous Great Heathen Army is a result of this.

In the end Sveinn *"Tjúguskegg"* Haraldsson (Sweyn Forkbeard) created the so-called North Sea Empire, ruling over all of Denmark, southern Sweden, southern Norway and Danelagen (a huge chunk of present day England).

The Dane Viking chieftain Hrólfr (Rolf or Rollo) was wearing down the Holy Roman Empire by attacking cities and monasteries in the river Seine, and even Paris, competing with other Vikings who did the same. The emperor struck a deal with him: By giving him the northern part of the country to rule, he would also become a buffer-state and protect the rest of the empire from further Viking raids.

This became a new country, a new group of Vikings and a new powerhouse: Normandy – the Normans who would attack and take over England only 19 days after the Danes were defeated.

To the east the situation was more stable. The Rus took over larger and larger parts of the area occupied by the Slavic tribes, always moving south towards the black sea, in order to address the great city of Miklagarðr, the capital in the Byzantine Empire.

With Birka, in Sweden, as the starting point Hrøríkr (Rurik) created a centre of power in Holmgarðr (Novgorod), by the important Dnieper river.

In 882 they moved the capital to Kyiv, hundreds of kilometres down the river, almost exactly midway between Birka and Miklagarðr.

They attacked Miklagarðr several times, but never succeeded in breaching the walls.

At the same time trading with the city continued, and after a number of attacks there was a peace treaty, resulting in the formation of the Varangian Guard; a special military unit made up by Rus Vikings serving the emperor.

Apparently people didn't hold grudges back then…

The Rus were ruling the Slavic people in Kievan Rus ruthlessly, but at the same time adapting exemplary to local customs, language, fashion, names, etc.

By inspiration – or force – from the Byzantines they adopted the Orthodox Christianity, and forced their Slavic subjects to do the same.

All these compromises and adaptations became the origin of the present day Ukrainian and Russian culture.

It may sound like a messy business, with every tool in the toolbox in use at the same time, but compared to the situation in the west it was a formidable show of stability.

VIKING WOMEN

Obviously the Iron Age society in Scandinavia was male dominated in many ways, but women nevertheless held many important positions in society that was affected in a very negative way with the introduction of Christianity.

Mediaeval Christianity was on one hand very strict (much more than we can imagine today), but on the other hand introduced slowly and in a very watered down edition in Scandinavia, so the loss of influence came gradually, over several generations.

As she would *"hold the fort"* at the farm when the husband was away on raiding or trading trips, the lady on the farm would in effect be the one who would give the final answer to any question regarding the farm – even when he was at home.

Women held much power in religious life, among other things as Völve (a female shaman).

Patronymic name giving has existed in Scandinavia until the 1800s, but before Christianity there were several examples of matronymes, like king Svend Estridsen and Sigurðr Áslaugsson.

So it seems like hardcore misogyny was introduced with Christianity.

But at the top of the power pyramid female rulers are easier to trace for historians and archaeologists than women at ordinary farms.

Graves of huge importance have been regarded as male (kings) as a reflex, until modern DNA analysis have made it possible to specify the gender, and this has been quite an eye opener.

The buried king in the famous Oseberg ship burial turned out to be a queen, and judging from the content of the grave perhaps one of the most important people in Iron Age Scandinavia.

Unfortunately we don't know anything about this person. There are many theories, but they are theories.

In Denmark it is obvious that both Gormr *"Gamli"* Hardeknudsson and his son Haraldr *"Blátǫnn"* Gormsson got their regal legitimacy from the wife and mother Þórvi *"Tannemark Bod"* Haraldrsdottir. She is mentioned on several runestones, and seems to be the real ruler of Denmark. The nickname *"Tannemark Bod"* can loosely be translated to *"Denmark's Pride"*.

The huge central grave mount in Jelling, Denmark, is made in her honour, and she is mentioned in both runestones on the ground. Around the grave mount is a symbolic stone marking of a gigantic ship, instead of a wooden ship inside the mount.

In Sweden an important warrior grave turned out to hold a woman, as well, and even if the background for the weapons present is still debated, there's no doubt she was important.

That brings us to the most powerful woman in Scandinavian history, who will get a whole chapter of her own somewhere else in this book: Helga of Kiev, who ruled the largest empire in Europe at that time.

Before we started using the title *"King"*, the title *"Drot"* was in use, in old Norse, to describe a sovereign ruler. The female equivalent to Drot is Drotning, and today the Scandinavian word for a queen is Dronning or Drottning. But Drotning originally didn't mean *"married to the king"*, but a ruler in her own right.

The way to become a female ruler, in a male dominated society, was by being the only heir to the throne, or by being the widow of a king – like Helga of Kiev.

But many women have ruled on behalf of a male child without being able to hold the title Drotning. One of the most famous in Europe is perhaps Margrete Valdemarsdatter, who ruled all of Scandinavia on behalf of her son, and when he died she quickly adopted a suitable heir, at such a young age, that she could continue to rule. Even when he came of age, she remained in *de facto* power, making sure he couldn't fuck it up until after her death. Which he did!

In the early 1970s the Danes had to make a hard choice, as the king left *"only"* daughters: Reinvent the Drotning as the actual ruler, or go for an intellectually challenged nephew. They chose the female ruler. She, in turn, chose the title Margrethe the second, in honour of Margrete Valdemarsdatter, in effect making her Drotning posthumously.

At a later point the Swedes made the same choice, though the Swedish king is still alive.

As Iceland is a republic they can't show off a queen, but they managed to elect the first female president in the world; Vigdís Finnbogadóttir, in 1980. With a presidency of exactly 16 years she is still the longest serving elected head of state of any country to date.

As we struggle to combat the effect of the introduction of mediaeval Christianity the Scandinavian countries are now regarded as the most gender equal in the world, according to the World Economic Forum and the United Nations Annual Reports on the subject.

We don't know if gender equality was a subject of debate in the Iron Age, but it's completely obvious from history and archaeology that women were regarded as much more important in the forn siðr society than in the mediaeval Christian society, even if women were actually one of the driving forces in the introduction of Christianity, like Helga of Kiev, and Þjóðhildur Jörundsdóttir, who were married to Eirikur *"Rauði"* Þorvaldsson (Eric the red) and build the first church in Brattalið (Greenland). Talk about shooting yourself in the food.

WERE THERE SHIELD-MAIDENS — FEMALE WARRIORS?

There is no doubt there have been fierce female warriors, but the evidence is rather blurry.

Warrior graves have been found and excavated, with assault axes, shields and swords, where the DNA proves the bones belonged to a woman.

This is not an answer, but the beginning of multiple questions.

Did she receive these grave gifts because she was a stand up member of society, did they belong to her husband, lost at war, did she fight to protect the village, while the men were away on raids, or did she actually participate in raids herself?

The answer can be yes to any of these questions, in any given grave.

We will presumably never know for sure.

A grave with weapons next to a female skeleton marked by injuries of war would be the proof we are waiting for, and that hasn't been found yet.
(This is disputed while I write this.)

The English, Frankish and Arab writers, who have described the Vikings in their own time, don't mention female warriors.

Obviously some women had to be able to handle weapons, since the village or farm would be vulnerable to attacks by sneaky neighbours when the men went on raids.

Although we don't know if she herself has swung an axe, you can look forward to reading the story about Helga of Kyiv!

DID THE IRON AGE VIKINGS PRACTISE POLYGAMY?

There doesn't seem to be a consensus. It must have been different from one place to the next.

Nothing indicates it has been a widespread practice.

The kings Svend Estridsen and Haraldr Hárfagri had impressive numbers of both wives, frills and children, but the overlapping is somewhat unclear.

COULD IRON AGE VIKINGS DIVORCE?

More than one contemporary source claims divorce was common, with horrified emphasis on women's rights to divorce.

Ibrahim ibn Yacoub Al-Tartushi famously wrote: *"they part with their husbands whenever they like"*.

Divorce amongst Æsir is even mentioned in the mythology, like Skaði divorcing Njörðr, and both Njörðr and Frigg are mentioned as Æsirs of divorce.

The practice disappeared as Christianity became the norm (c.1100), and returned as Christianity faded (c.1950).

It is rumoured that Scandinavian countries are now among the nations in the world with the highest divorce rate, but this is not true as they are ranked 20 (Sweden), 22 (Denmark), 39 (Iceland) and 46 (Norway) below countries such as Egypt, Kazakhstan and China.

IRON AGE VIKINGS AND LGBT+?

It is the general perception that most Vikings were very open minded and curious in most subjects, but to claim that we know their attitude towards LGBT+ is stretching it too far.

We have archaeological excavations, sagas and chronicles, and none of them mention LGBT+ specifically, so it would be a wild guess.

In mythology, some deities change gender both ways.

Loki is an example: He changes into a female creature and gives birth to three offspring.

In the sagas some male or female friendships are described in ways that could hint bi- or homosexuality, but we have to remember how descriptions and attitudes change over time, and over distances.

Is it a romance or a bromance?

As an example of how easy you can get confused I will mention how common it is for north African men to hold hands with their male friends, while walking the streets, and simultaneously having a very anxiety-ridden perception of homosexuality.

Now we are talking about people living a thousand years ago... People who didn't even have a word for homosexuality.

In the chronicles priests and monks describe all the things they dislike about Vikings, and they never mention LGBT+.

So: We don't know!

HAVE THERE BEEN ARAB OR AFRICAN VIKINGS?

This is where it gets blurry for real, and we have to go back to the initial question: *"What is a Viking?"*.

Some slaves have raised to become ordinary members of society, and participated in raids.

A handful of these can have been Arabs or African.

Many Rus Vikings served in the Byzantine Varangian Guard, no doubt side by side with Byzantine warriors from other parts of the empire.

And groups of Vikings have in countless instances allied with local people on their raids and conquests.

It's vitally important to remember that most rulers in history have been some kind of tyrants, and parts of the population will therefore regard any attacker on their land as liberators.

The Vikings were masters of finding the weak links, the suppressed people, the frustrated subjects, and forming alliances.

That's how 800 Vikings could conquer an entire country. So Vikings have without a shred of doubt been fighting side by side with both Arabs and Africans.

But being an ally with Vikings doesn't necessarily make you a Viking.

So let's just say *"Yes, there must have been some, but most likely only a handful."*

DID THE VIKINGS TAKE SLAVES?

Yes they did.

Slavery was actually the primary foundation for the Viking expansion.

In some cases it would in effect be kidnapping, as the family would buy them free on the spot, but most were taken to the great slave markets in Dublin, Jórik (York), Birka, Heiðabýr, Kyiv or Miklagarðr (Constantinople).

Dublin and Heiðabýr are actually founded on the Viking slave trade.

Slaves in the Iron Age were called *"trælle"* (thralls), but the word *"slave"* probably derives from the fact that many of the slaves came from the Slavic tribes.

Besides the slave trade with foreign nations the Viking them selves had slaves in almost every farm.

They lived as a subdued part of the family, and often slept under the same roof as their owners, but most oftenly in the opposite end of the house, with the livestock.

In some cases slaves were allowed to make money, and could buy their freedom.

In other cases slaves would be made free through marriage or adoption.

There are even cases where people volunteered to become slaves, in order to survive famine.

I'm not trying to sugar coat it: Being a slave was degrading, hard work, tough living conditions, and an easy target for violence and any kind of abuse, including rape.

We only hear about the slaves who rose to the top of the society, never the hundreds of thousands who died young and broken down.

In Denmark the word *"træls"* (slave-like) is still used about everything that is annoying or hard.

WHAT HAVE THE IRON AGE VIKINGS LEFT FOR THE PRESENT?

INTERNATIONALLY

In many languages originating in northern Europe the weekdays are named after the Æsir.

Lots of words in modern English, like wife, knife, son, daughter, eggs, sky, etc.

Christmas traditions, like not fasting, but rather eating too much, decorating with fir branches and fruit.

New year's resolutions.

Numerous history-inspired and saga-inspired movies from History Channel to Marvel, and everything in between.

Artistic influence in interior design, patterns etc.

The ship design is carried through to today, where important design features can be found in even the largest container vessels in the ocean.

But most importantly, of course, the invention of the modern parliament – *"Altinget"*. Without it representative democracy wouldn't work.

Vikings have even founded several cities, including Dublin, and regions, like Normandy.

And let's not forget how they have inspired *"Der Ring des Nibelungen"* by Richard Wagner, and *"The Lord of the Rings"* by J.R.R. Tolkien.

The Vikings conquered England in the Iron Age, and England conquered the world during the Age of Discovery, spreading our weird habits and customs.

IN SCANDINAVIA

In Scandinavia it's obviously everywhere.

Half of all children's names, most village and city names, many streets and squares.

Denmark, which is a completely flat archipelago, has all these tiny hills, scattered all over the landscape, typically 25 metres across, five to ten metres tall. You see them everywhere, and small children use them to slide down on snowy winter days. These are graves from the Viking Age, and before.

Scandinavian children are raised with the stories about the Æsir, and all their mischiefs.

Even the extraordinary number of pigs and herrings finding their way to plates around Scandinavia has its roots in the Iron Age.

The language is of course rooted in the ancient Norse, and even words that should make little sense in the modern age, is used frequently, like *"jätte"*, in Swedish, that originally meant giant (jǫtunn), in folk tales, and the word *"træls"*, in Danish, that was the Viking word for slave labour.

In design, which is still considered an important part of Scandinavian claim to fame, there is a strong focus on the use of natural materials, endurance, and multiple uses.
Is it a jug or a vase? Is it a cutting board or a serving dish?
In Scandinavia these are stupid questions, and the answer is obviously *"yes"*.

Scandinavians have this Viking spirit that makes us open-minded and generally well mannered, but at the same time strangely insensitive to all things irrational, like religious dogma and the family's *"honour"*.

A teenage daughter being seen drunk and naked on the beach would perhaps constitute a crisis in a Saudi Arabian family, but I couldn't care less.

And last, but not least: Are you familiar with the word *"Hygge"*?

The Vegvisir (The Guide) is a magical symbol intended to help the bearer find their way. The symbol is attested in the Huld Manuscript, collected in Iceland by Geir Vigfusson in 1860, and does not have any earlier attestations.

THE VIKING COUNTRIES NOW

Even though Greenland and Sweden are fairly easy to spot on the map, it's safe to say the Viking countries are now micronations.

Big brother Sweden has only 10 million inhabitants, Denmark 5.8, Norway 5.4, Iceland 370,000, Greenland 57,000 and the Faroe Islands 53,000.

Armies and navies are very low priorities.

Being raided or occupied by a Viking army should not be at the top of your list of worries.

Borders have been moved around like a weird board game, as the original power player, Denmark, lost ground to Sweden.

Later division became a thing, where Norway, Finland and Iceland gained independence, in 1905, 1917 and 1944.

Greenland and the Faroe Islands are still semi-detached colonies to Denmark.

The years of having influence in England, France, Russia and Ukraine are definitely over.

The only reminiscent of the great Viking fleet is the Danish shipping company Mærsk.

Taking slaves and setting the world on fire has been substituted with IKEA and Carlsberg.

When it comes to landscapes you want to go to Norway, as that is the country of dramatic vertical mountains and deep fjords. Sweden is one big forest, and Denmark is a completely(!) flat archipelago of beaches and fields.

In Iceland you'll find volcanoes and the northern light, and in the Faroe Islands everything is hidden in the fog.

Greenland is grand and breathtaking, but it's impossible to get around.

All over Scandinavia you will see the small grassy hills that are burial mounds from the past.

Many cities, squares and streets are named in the historic Viking Age, and you can have a few giggles about what you'll find in *"Odin's Parking Space"*, or whether *"Miklagårdsväg"* will actually take you all the way to Istanbul.

In Denmark you'll find the mediaeval church architecture to be self-explanatory: They are not made for worship but to be defended. Religion has always been more about politics than faith.

When it comes to architecture, language, and the minor details in the culture, you will observe the logical effects of geography: Denmark is most *"Pan-European"*, Sweden a little less so, but somewhat influenced by Slavic culture, Norway is more independently Scandinavian, and Iceland is completely cut off from the continent, still learning runes in school, and using patronymic last names.

VIKINGS AND CULTURAL APPROPRIATION?

It happens I meet Scandinavians who bite their knuckles because of Americans making Viking reenactment, blóting to Óðinn etc.

That can be perceived as double standards amplified to the max.

Viking culture during the Iron Age was the very epitome of cultural appropriation!

Not only did the Vikings *"go native"* as soon as they arrived at a new location, they brought home ideas, tools, fashion, food, superstitions, stories and recipes, by the shipload, and made them their own.

The Viking Culture was – and still is – a living, growing, constantly changing organism, with several offsprings.

The Rus laid the ground for the modern Russian culture, the Danes and the Normans laid the foundation for the modern English culture, and the influence has spread throughout the world, to the extent where you speak old Norse when you say *"wife"* (and about 2000 other words), and you are celebrating Norse pagan traditions when you decorate with fir branches for Christmas.

But it wasn't a one way deal, and if you visited a Scandinavian farm in the year 1000 you would find influences and inventions from almost the entire northern hemisphere.

If you ask a Pechenegs *"who made you Christian?"* he will obviously reply *"the Vikings did!"*.

If we could revive a 1000 years old Viking, would he eat Tom Yum and use a smartphone? Oh, yes, in a heartbeat.

That's the way the world works, and if we are allowed to have Taco Friday, maybe we should let the Americans hold a blót.

The only point where it turns self-contradictory is when nutcases appropriate a Viking icon and use it to promote a nationalistic, culture conservative, or even racist idea.

That unfortunately happens, not only in the USA, but even in Sweden there's a neo-nazi group named *"Nordic Resistance Movement"* that uses the T rune as their logo.

An extreme example of *not* being familiar with your own history, and as so often is the case, the people struggling for ethnic purity are the least appealing members of that specific ethnic group – both when it comes to moral standards and intellectual capacities.

WHAT IS NORDICISM?

"Nordicists" are an unforgivably simple-minded group of morons.

"Nordicism" surfaced for the first time in the 1930's.

It's the belief that Scandinavians are a purebred superior ethnic group that should rule the world, or at least be left alone to stay *"uncontaminated"*.

Hitler used this in his propaganda, and now neo-nazis, like Nordiska Motståndsrörelsen (*"Nordic Resistance Movement"*) or Jacob Chansley, the self-proclaimed *"QAnon Shaman"* from Arizona, and countless others, are doing the same.

Obviously they haven't read anything about Vikings before deciding that they are: Tall, blond, strong, violent, homophobic, racist misogynists.

Let us get this straight:

Many Vikings were tall. Some were not.

Some Vikings were blond. Most were not.

Most were strong, like everybody else working hard with primitive tools. That wasn't uniquely the Vikings…

The Vikings were hyper violent – in a hyper violent time.

Homophobic? We don't really know, but they did blót to Æsir that was gender-fluid…

Racist? Ethnicists?
The concepts of *"race"* and *"ethnicity"* weren't invented. A different skin colour was a curiosity, nothing more or less. Hostility, alliances and slavery took place without distinction of ethnic groups, skin colours, language and religion

Misogynists? Well, it was a patriarchal society, but women were held in higher esteem in the Iron Age, than in the centuries that followed. Misogyny was imported from other parts of Europe.

In the late 1990s and early 2000s, there was a tendency for Scandinavians to refrain from using Viking symbols – and even their own flag – so as not to be mistaken for mentally disabled racists.

Fortunately, this trend has changed and normal healthy people have taken back the symbols.

However, there is an exception: The swastika, which was used by the Vikings (as well as Romans, Indians and others), and was the logo of the Danish brewery Carlsberg, is no longer used. It got too inflamed.

VIKING:STORIES

HELGA OF KYIV

PRESUMED HISTORICAL ACCURACY: 70%.

Rus Vikings – or Sveas – from the area around Lake Mälaren, with important cities like Birka and Uppsala, found a way into the Dnieper river on the other side of the Baltic Sea, and went on countless expeditions for raiding and trading already in the bronze age, and perhaps even earlier.

In 862 Hrøríkr (Rurik) established himself as the ruler of Holmgarðr (Novgorod), and became the founder of a dynasty that would rule Russia and Ukraine until 1610, where Tzar Vasili IV died as the last of the Rurik Dynasty.

Hrøríkr's son Ingvarr Hrøríkrsson (Igor Rurikovich) moved the capital from Holmgarðr to Kyiv, and married Helga.

We know almost nothing about Helga's early life or background, except that she was about 15 years old when she married prince Ingvarr.

But we will get to hear about her, and then some!

In 945 Ingvarr was killed by the Drevlian Prince Mal, while collecting taxes, and left Helga with a three year old son, and heir to the throne.

Shortly after, Prince Mal sent twenty soldiers to ask for her hand in marriage. After all, a woman can't rule alone…

According to legend she asked them to wait in their boat, until the next day, when they would be carried to her court in the boat, as a special honour.

The next day they were indeed carried in the boat, and thought that this was a great honour, until they were dropped into a trench, dug the previous day on Helga's order.

It is written that Helga bent down to watch them as they were buried and *"inquired whether they found the honour to their taste."*

Helga then sent a message to the Drevlians that they should send *"their distinguished men to her in Kyiv, so that she might go to their Prince with due honour."*

The Drevlians, unaware of the fate of the first diplomatic party, gathered another party of men to send *"the best men who governed the land of Dereva."*

When they arrived, Helga commanded her people to draw them a bath and invited the men to appear before her after they had bathed. When the Drevlians entered the bath-house, Helga had it set on fire from the doors, so that all the Drevlians within burned to death.

Helga then sent another messenger to Prince Mal, asking him to prepare a great wedding party.

As she arrived with a small following of Rus Vikings Prince Mal was wondering why she was arriving before the rather large Drevlian escort, but was informed they would follow soon.

He had no idea the first group had been buried alive, and the second burned to death.

Also he had no idea that the group that would *"follow soon"* was in fact a quite substantial group of Rus warriors.

The feast began, and as co-host Helga made sure there was enough alcohol being served.

Late at night all the guests were extremely drunk, and Helga gave signals to the Rus warriors who had surrounded the city.

According to the Primary Chronicle, five thousand Drevlians were killed on this night, but Helga returned to Kyiv to prepare an army to finish off the survivors.

As the Drevlian country became absorbed by Kievan Rus, only one city was a serious obstacle: Iskorosten, where Ingvarr had been killed. The residents thought that they would not survive, so they protected the city walls at all costs.

The siege lasted for a year without success when Helga thought of a plan to trick the Drevlians.

She told them to catch and give her all the sparrows from the city, as a token of goodwill, and she would spare their lives.

Happy to see the end of the troubles they did as she asked.

Helga then instructed her army to attach a piece of sulphur bound with small pieces of cloth to each bird. At nightfall, Helga told her soldiers to set the pieces aflame and release the birds. They returned to their nests within the city, which subsequently set the city ablaze.

As the Primary Chronicle tells it: *"There was not a house that was not consumed, and it was impossible to extinguish the flames, because all the houses caught fire at once."*

As the people fled the burning city, Helga ordered her soldiers to catch them, killing some of them and giving the others as slaves to her followers.

Her late husband Ingvarr had besieged Miklagarðr twice, in 941 and 944, and although Greek fire (napalm) destroyed part of his fleet, he concluded a favourable treaty with the Byzantine Emperor Constantine VII in 945.

Some time in the 950s Helga visited Constantinople, where she was received by the emperor.

With a lustful eye fixed on the Kievan Rus empire, he asked Helga to marry him.

She told him that she was a pagan, and would only convert to Christianity if she was baptised by the Patriarch, and with the emperor as her sponsor and godfather.

Converting Kievan Rus to Christianity was a good offer, but it would also prevent the emperor from taking control through marriage, as it would be illegal to marry his god-daughter, by the rules of the Christian church.

She outsmarted him, but he agreed to the arrangement, where Helga took the Christian name Helena (or Elena).

After all the arrangement had mutual benefits, as the common religion would help secure continued trade and a steady supply of slaves, fur, amber and other precious commodities from Kievan Rus, and Helga left with gold, silver, silks, and various vases.

Back in Kyiv she started building churches and campaigning for the conversion to Christianity.

Some of her less supporting subjects were forced to convert, while close allies could choose as they saw fit.

Her own son, Sveinald Ingvarsson (Sviatoslav the Brave) refused, and stayed a pagan for the entirety of his life, but gave his mother, Helga, a Christian burial.

He reigned over the Kievan Rus' for ten years, a reign that was marked by rapid expansion into the Volga River valley, the Pontic steppe, and the Balkans. By the end of his short life, Sveinald carved out for himself the largest state in Europe. He was ambushed and slain by the Pechenegs in 972. The Chronicle reports that his skull was made into a chalice by the Pecheneg khan.

His youngest, and illegitimate, son, Valdemar Sveinaldsson (Vladimir the Great), born by the housekeeper Malusha, became a Christian, and proclaimed Christianity to be the official religion of Kievan Rus in 988, after a great deal of shopping around for a religion.

This at the same time he had to fight (and kill) his older siblings for power, as he was last in line for the throne.

First he tried to reform Slavic paganism in an attempt to identify himself with the various gods worshipped by his subjects. He built a pagan temple on a hill in Kiev with Norse, Slavic, Finnish and Persian Gods. At the same time he invited missionaries from Islam, Roman Catholicism, Judaism, and Byzantine Orthodoxy.

Finally he chose the last, which was probably the best political choice for future defence and trade.

Sometime in the 1200s Helga of Kyiv, baptised as Helena (or Elena), and known to Slavic speaking people as Olga, was canonised by the Orthodox Church as Saint Helena or Saint Olga, and later she became recognized as the national saint of Russia and Ukraine; *"Equal to the Apostles"*.

Reading her life story and achievements it's quite obvious she holds all the virtues of a Christian saint.

Later her grandson, Vladimir the Great was canonised as well.

THE VENGEANCE OF RAGNARR'S SONS

PRESUMED HISTORICAL ACCURACY: 1%

The Swedish princess Þora got a small snake as a child, and asked her father how she could make it grow, as it was only the size of her hand.

He told her that she should give it a gold coin to lay on. She did so, and the snake grew a little. The next day she gave it another coin, and it grew a little more. As she came into adulthood the snake was now a full grown dragon.

(Note: Dragons in Viking mythology are not winged fire spewing beasts, but large snakes or serpents.)

Her father said that whoever could kill the dragon would get his daughter's hand, and all the gold, and be the heir to the kingdom.

Ragnarr had some furry trousers made that could protect him against the venom from the snake, and killed it. As a proof he left the spearhead in the serpent's head, so everyone could see that only his shaft would match the spearhead.

(A little Cinderella detail there…)

Furry trousers is *"Loðbrók"* in old Norse.

That is the story of how he got his name and became the king of Sweden, while in other stories he is the son of the Swedish king.

He is also the king of Denmark and Norway, in case you wonder.

After Þora died, he discovered Kráka, a woman of outstanding beauty and wisdom living with a poor peasant couple in Norway, and married her. This marriage resulted in the sons

Ívarr *"Hinn Beinlausi"* Ragnarsson, Björn Járnsíða, Halfdan *"Hvítserkr"* Ragnarsson, Ragnvald, Ubbe and Sigurðr *"Ormr í auga"* Áslaugsson.

Kráka was later revealed to actually be Áslaug, a secret daughter of the renowned hero Sigurðr Fafnesbane (Dragon-slayer).

As the sons grew up to become renowned warriors, Ragnarr, not wishing to be outdone, resolved to conquer England with merely two ships. He was however defeated by superior English forces and thrown into a snake pit to die in agony, by king Ælla of Northumberland.

Áslaug, who was a Völve, had made a magical shirt for him that protected him from the snake's bite and venom, so they had to drag him out of the hole to undress him, before throwing him in again, and seeing him die.

He held a longer speech about going proudly to Valhǫll, and said *"How the little piggies will grunt when they hear how the old boar suffered."*

This remark would serve to provoke the sons to man up, when they heard of his death.

According to the saga, avenging his death was the reason for the formation of *"The Great Heathen Army"*.

According to middle age Danish historians Ragnarr *"Loðbrók"* Sigurðsson fathered Sigurðr *"Ormr í auga"* Áslaugsson who fathered Hardeknud Sigurðsson > Gormr *"Gamli"* Hardeknudsson > Haraldr *"Blótan"* Gormsson > Svein *"Tjúguskegg"* Haraldsson > Knútr *"Ínn ríki"* Sveinsson and so on. The last four are without doubt actual people, and forefathers to the present royal family in Denmark.

HARALDR "HARÐRÁÐI" SIGURÐARSON

<u>PRESUMED HISTORICAL ACCURACY: 90%</u>

To English historians Haraldr *"Harðráði"* Sigurðarson (Harald Hårderåde, loosely translatable to Harald Badass) was the last real Viking king.

He was born in 1015 to the Earl Sigurdar Syr, and participated in his first battle at the age of 15, at Stiklestad.

The battle was between the Danish king Knútr *"Ínn ríki"* Sveinsson (Cnut the Great) and Haraldr's own half-brother Olav II Haraldsson.

Haraldr was on the losing side of the battle, and had to escape.

First he went to Kiev, where he found protection at the court of Jarizleifr Valdemarsson (Yaroslav the Wise), the son of Valdemar Sveinaldsson (Vladimir the Great) (see the story about Helga of Kyiv).

After a while he needed to raise some cash, so he left for Miklagarðr in order to join the Varangian Guard.

He fought and made himself famous in the Mediterranean, Asia Minor, Sicily, the Holy Land and Bulgaria.

Rich on experience and money he went back to Scandinavia in 1046, where he immediately became a part of intrigues and power struggles, as the Norwegian-Danish king Magnus the Good fought against the Danish earl Svend Estridsen.

Haraldr and Svend joined forces, but when Magnus offered Haraldr to become co-king, he failed Svend.

Shortly afterwards, in 1047, Magnus died. Possibly from the injuries he sustained when he pursued Svend after a battle on Zealand and reportedly fell from his horse. Magnus gave Norway to Harald and Denmark to Svend.

Haraldr and Svend met many times in battles in the following years; both on land and at sea.

Haraldr plundered and burned Heiðabýr in 1049, just as he ravaged many other places in Denmark. The Skuldelev barrier over Roskilde Fjord, the first part of which is believed to be from c. 1060, is often interpreted as an attempt to secure Roskilde against Haraldr's surprise attack. Although much of Haraldr's rampage seems aimless, he was probably too great a strategist to simply go on random raids. Perhaps the purpose was to show how Svend could not protect his coasts, and thus remove the Danes' support for him.

Despite the fact that Svend Estridsen lost virtually every battle between him and Haraldr, he managed to hold on to power, and they entered into a settlement in 1062. The warrior king Haraldr must have realised that he had to find new hunting grounds, and after the death of the English King Edward the Confessor at the beginning of 1066, Haraldr invaded England. Here, however, he died the same autumn, September 26th, in the Battle of Stamford Bridge against the new English king, Harold Godwinson.

His death marks, according to English historians, the end of the Viking Age.

THE GREENLANDERS

<u>PRESUMED HISTORICAL ACCURACY: 80%.</u>

Naddoðr discovered a new uninhabited island, named it Snow Island, and left for the Faroe Islands without making any further effort to explore it.

Word got around, and later *"Hrafna"*-Flóki Vilgerðarson was leading the first attempt to populate the island, and failed completely. According to legend he was the one who came up with the name Iceland.

Eventually people started moving in, and developing the farming skills to survive on the island.

Þórvaldr Ásvaldsson, the great great grandson of Naddoðr killed a man in Norway in the 950s, and at that time murder didn't necessarily carry the death penalty. To avoid endless vendettas it had become customary to exile people for murder, so Þórvaldr and his extended family moved to Iceland, for a fresh start.

The apple falls close to the tree, and in the 970s his son Eiríkur *"Rauði"* Þorvaldsson (Eric the Red) killed a man in a dispute, and was exiled.

This led him to travel further north and west, and made him discover new land that he would name Greenland for one or two reasons.

First of all this was in the warm part of the middle ages, and the first sight of the coast may actually have presented huge green slopes.

Secondly it was guaranteed to fetch the attention of people living in Iceland.

In the end his efforts led to the establishments of two settlements in Greenland, the west and the east settlement. Both are actually on the west coast, but one of them is slightly more east, as it is placed on the southern coast. Naming them the northern and the southern would make a lot more sense.

The settlements thrived, and there was actually quite a lot of trade with both Iceland and Norway, as the Greenlanders could provide luxury articles like fur from seal, arctic fox and polar bear, and ivory from walrus.

At the same time Inuits have started moving south, until they stood face to face with Vikings, and the meeting seems to have been peaceful, and skills have been exchanged.

The problem, however, was that they were definitely not self-sufficient, as Greenland has no trees.

In the late 980s Bjarni Herjólfsson tried to get to Greenland, to find his father, and was blown off course.

To his amazement he found something that didn't resonate with the descriptions he had heard of Greenland.

As he finally managed to find the right settlement in Greenland he could tell what he had seen further to the west: Trees as tall as mountains, and a much more lush climate.

His words didn't fall on deaf ears, and the following years some exploration expeditions must have been made, though they are never recorded.

In year 1000 the son and daughter of Eiríkur *"Rauði"* Þorvaldsson, Leifur *"Heppni"* Eiríksson and Freydís Eiríksdóttir, set out to colonise the new land they had named Vinland (Wine Land), in the present day Gulf of Saint

Lawrence, in Canada. They brought a following of c. 50 people.

Traces of their presence are still visible in present day L'Anse aux Meadows.

In 1050 the Vikings disappeared from Vinland, and in c. 1400 they disappeared from Greenland.

There are literally hundreds of speculations and theories, but the truth is: We don't know why, in any of these cases.

One of the more colourful theories why the Vikings left Vinland is that they developed a good relation to the locals (even they called them *"Skrällinger"* (cowards or weaklings)), but when they got really friendly they made the mistake of serving them cow's milk. The indigenous population in America are lactose intolerant, and may have thought the Vikings tried to poison them, and the following conflict made the Vikings flee for their lives.

The reason why or how they disappeared from Greenland are often more serious.

One of them is the simple fact that the establishment of the settlements were in the hot period of the middle age, and their disappearance matches the cold period (the so-called *"little ice age"*).

Another theory is that they lost all trade connections because of better and cheaper ivory from Africa, combined with the plague in Europe.

In the more colourful end of the scale they were massacred by the Inuits or taken slaves by raiders from Portugal.

In the 1700s there was a renewed interest in their fate, and popular rumours suggested their descendants lived in isolation somewhere in Greenland. In 1721 the Danish priest

Hans Egede went to Greenland to find and re-establish the Norse colonies. He discovered no survivors of the old colonists, but he stayed to found his own settlement at Godthåb (now Nuuk).

Iceland, on the other hand, has been inhabited continuously since the first successful settlement, and thanks to the Landnámabók and the Íslendingabók we have the names of each and everyone recorded to this day.

MYTHOLOGY

ÆSIR AND VANIR – THE NORSE GODS

Even though the Vikings were Christened in the middle of the Viking Age, and became predominantly atheist in modern times, the Norse religion (Asatro/forn siðr) still exists. There are only a very small minority of active followers, but the names and the stories are a vital part of Scandinavian history and everyday culture.

In Scandinavia you'll see Mjölnír, and tról figures everywhere, and many places are named accordingly, like the city Oðense in Denmark, and my youngest daughter's daycare centre Miðgården.

As a child I firmly believed the thunder was the work of Þórr, and so did my children.

Their children will come to believe it too.

Labelling the Æsir and Vanir *"Gods"* is slightly incorrect, as they are physical and mortal beings, even though they have supernatural and magical abilities, and live for thousands of years.

Æsir, Vanir and Jǫtunn are not – as many think – different races or species, as they so often change from one to the other, or have children with each other.

The same way it's worth mentioning that Dwarfs and Elves are the result of bad translations to English, as they both are Elves in the ancient Norse language – Black Elves and Light Elves.

YGGDRASIL – THE WORLD TREE

The world is made up of the world tree, Yggdrasil, and in pre-modern times, before the light pollution, you could see the canopy in the sky at night (as the Milky Way).

The tree has nine roots, containing the nine worlds, or nine dimensions.

Yggdrasil doesn't have a fixed size, and can be as small as any normal tree or as large as the known universe.

ÁSGARÐR

Ásgarðr is the land of the Æsir, where you will find many great halls, including the famous Valhǫll (or *"Valhalla"*).

All the Æsir have their mansions here.

Even Freyja and Freyr, who are not Æsir, but Vanir, live here, as a guarantee for peace, after the mighty war between Æsir and Vanir.

The word *"garð"* can be translated to *"farm"*, *"estate"* or even *"land"*.

MIÐGARÐR

Miðgarðr is the world where humans live. It is round, like a ball, and surrounding it you will find Miðgarðsormr (the Miðgarðr snake), which bites its own tail to create a perfect circle.

Everything that is round can somehow represent Miðgarðr, whether it's a circle or a ball.

ÚTGARÐAR AND JOTUNHEIMR

Jǫtunn (*"The Giants"*) lives in Jǫtunheimr, most of them inside the grand fortress Útgarðar. The place is enormous, and so are jǫtunn.

They have magical powers and they are shape shifters, so you can meet one that is very small and beautiful, because they trick you.

Jǫtunn are evil, narrow-minded, small-minded and craving. They have no moral virtues.

Jǫtunn almost never visits Miðgarðr, but they are constantly trying to get into Ásgarðr because they want what the Æsir have.

TRÓLS

Tróls are a kind of jǫtunn that are exiled from Jǫtunheimr, and live in Miðgarðr. They seek solitude and can be dangerous if disturbed.

SVARTALFHEIMR

The Black Elves (also known as dwarfs) are small, ugly and intolerant to daylight, but they are amazing craftsmen, and they can add magic properties to the items they make, like weapons and jewellery.

Svartalfheimr (literally *"Black Elves' Home"*) is an entire world inside a mountain.

ÁLFHEIMR

The light Elves home.

The Light Elves are related but somehow opposed to the black elves.

They are good and gentle, and possess magic powers that create symbiosis in nature.

They are never introduced individually, so even if some people think they are equal to Æsir and Vanir, we don't know any names or personalities.

To add to the confusion Freyr's home in Ásgarðr(?) is sometimes mentioned as Álfheimr.

BIFRÖST

Bifröst is the invisible bridge that connects the nine worlds. It will be visible when the rain is followed by sunshine, as the rainbow. Only the Æsir and Vanir can use the bridge, and at one end of the bridge, in Ásgarðr, Heimdallr will stand guard to make sure no one enters without permission.

GIMLE

Much like the Christian and Muslim heaven, Gimle is the world where all good humans and Æsir will be welcomed after Ragnarǫk.

It's a place of peace and tranquillity.

THE WOLF FENRISÚLFR

Just like Miðgarðsormr Fenrisúlfr is a freak offspring of Loki.

A cute little wolf puppy, adored by the Æsir.

But he didn't stop growing, and became a monstrosity that destroyed everything in his path.

The Æsir tried to tie him down with larger and larger chains, presenting it to Fenrisúlfr as a challenge. He broke them all.

In the end they made the black elves create a chain of magic stuff, very thin and delightful, called Gleipnir.

Fenrisúlfr understood that he was being tricked, and would only test it if Týr would have one arm in his mouth. When he realised that he couldn't break free from Gleipne he bit off Týr's arm.

VANAHEIMR

This is where the Vanir lives, the other group of deities, associated with wisdom, and the ability to see the future. We know nothing about them until we meet in Gimle after Ragnarǫk.

Except for Njörðr, Freyja and Freyr, who live in Ásgarðr, and have thus revealed themselves.

NORNS

The Norns spin the threads of fate at the foot of Yggdrasil, the tree of the world. The threads represent lives, and the length of the individual thread determines the length of a person's life.

You can still hear, at a funeral in Scandinavia, someone saying *"His thread wasn't longer than this"*.

NISSE/TOMTE

A Nisse (Danish) or Tomte (Swedish) is a supernatural being that lives on every farm. They can be helpful or annoying, depending on how you treat them.

They are small, often described as about 40 cm, and the usual descriptions of their appearance has inspired the garden gnome.

They hide as best as they can, and hate to be spotted by humans.

FÓLKVANGR, VALHOLL AND HELHEIMR – THE AFTERLIFE

In modern popular culture it's common to hear Vikings longing to go to Valhǫll, almost like the ultimate paradise.

That is a misunderstanding.

The best and most courageous warriors will be hand-picked by Freyja for Fólkvangr.

The rest of them will go to Valhǫll.

Those who lived and died insignificant will oftenly go to Helheimr, a dark and dull place where nothing happens (not to be confused with Hell, where one is punished and burned. That's a different religion.)

Some sagas even tell of Niflheim, where everything is frozen, surrounding Helheimr.

But there are a number of other places humans can go in the afterlife, including the home of Gefion, which is a sanctuary for virgins.

These places are however temporary, as they will all vanish in Ragnarǫk.

After Ragnarǫk the good Æsir and humans will be welcomed in Gimle.

RAGNAROK

Ragnarǫk starts with the death of Baldr.

The wolves that have been hunting the sun and the moon since the beginning of time will finally catch and swallow them.

Fimbulvintr will follow, where the world freezes over.

The bridge Bifröst will fall apart, and the wolf Fenrisúlfr will break free.

The Miðgarðr snake will twist and turn, and the oceans will flood Miðgarðr.

All the different Æsir, Vanir, the warriors from Fólkvangr and Valhǫll, who has practised for this every day, will meet jǫtunn, the wolf Fenrisúlfr and the Miðgarðr snake in a final battle.

Everybody dies in the battle, and the world goes down in flames.

Silence and darkness follows.

Like a dawning the great hall Gimle will rise of the nothingness, and welcome all who have been good.

ÓÐINN

Óðinn (*"Odin"*, *"Oden"* or *"Woden"*) is the main áss, according to most traditions.

He is somehow the originator of all the other Æsir, and therefore sometimes referred to as the *"Allfather"*.

Other nicknames are *"The Tall One"* and *"The One Eyed"*.

According to legends he gave one of his eyes to Mímir, as a payment for drinking from the well of wisdom that Mímir guards.

Other variations tell that he left his eye in the well as a remote way of seeing wisdom.

Óðinn has two ravens – Hugin and Munin – that will fly out in the world to spy for him. If you see a raven there's a fair chance the Allfather is keeping an eye on you.

He also owns Sleipner, an eight legged horse that can run very fast on land, on water and even in the air.

His most profound property might be his magical spear Gugner.

Óðinn seeks wisdom at all costs, and is not necessarily invested in your best interests.

Óðinn has more than 200 different nicknames, among them Julfadern – a little tongue in cheek translatable to *"Father Christmas"*.

He once sacrificed himself (to himself, somehow) by hanging himself from a tree for nine days. For that reason he is (among many other things) the áss for the hanged, and for suiciders.

He is also the áss for *"skjalde"* (poetry and music) and for wisdom and learning.

Óðinn is the (natural) father of Baldr and Þórr.

He is married to Frigg, in some traditions, and Freyja in others.

ÞÓRR

Þórr (*"Thor"* or *"Tor"*) is the áss for humans, and a son of Óðinn.

In some traditions he is the main áss, as Adam of Bremen described the huge statue of Þórr, centre stage, in the temple hall in Uppsala, flanked by two minor statues of Óðinn and Freyr.

Þórr's most prized possession is no doubt his magical war hammer, that will never miss a target, and will return to his hand after being thrown.

The hammer's name is Mjölnír (or *"Mjølner"*), and used by many heathens in necklaces, in much the same way as Christians use the cross; for protection and identification.

Þórr mainly uses the hammer for killing jǫtunn, and keep Ásgarðr safe.

Along with Óðinn and Týr he is a Æsir of war, defence and protection, but for humans he has many roles and functions.

Þórr can be quite a fool, at times, and many stories are about silly mistakes and embarrassing situations he got himself into.

According to some historians Þórr is a rather late addition to the pantheon, as he was unknown in the bronze age.

FREYJA

Love and death are the two main areas of interest for this beautiful young and endlessly attractive ásynja.

Or is she?

The black elves made her a magical necklace Brisingamén that will make everyone see her as irresistibly desirable.

She lives in her estate Fólkvangr, where she keeps an army of magical female warriors called Valkyries.

After a battle the Valkyries will fly down to the battlefield and finish off the dying warriors, and bring all the dead to Freyja, who will pick and choose.

The best and most courageous she will of course keep for herself, other heroes will go to Valhǫll, and the rest will be sent to Hel.

She has a cart dragged by two huge cats, but for war she will ride her wild boar Hildisvíni.

Freyja is one of the Vanir living in Ásgarðr.

She is the daughter of Njörðr and brother of Freyr.

She is married to Od, in some traditions, and Óðinn in others.

Freyja was especially targeted by the Christian missionaries and priests when the Vikings were christened, since she represents virtues like female lust and extramarital sex.

FREYR

Freyr is a Vanir, son of Njörðr, and brother of Freyja.

In very old traditions he is both brother and husband to Freyja, as that was customary among Vanir.

Overlapping traditions claim that they were married but forced to divorce when they were sent to Ásgarðr as hostages, following the great Æsir-Vanir war. Brother-sister marriage is not acceptable in Ásgarðr or Miðgarðr.

Freyr is sometimes associated with agriculture, and offerings (blót) to Freyr could secure a successful harvest.

TÝR

Týr is a warrior áss, along with Óðinn and Þórr.

The "*T*" rune (↑) is often associated with him, and used to secure victory.

Unfortunately some very misguided neo Nazis in Scandinavia also use his rune as their logo.

It is not the first time Vikings have been used in association with racism, which is weird when you get to understand Viking history.

(You can live a very happy life without having the slightest clue about history, but you will give the rest of us a serious migraine!)

FRIGG

Óðinn's wife, according to some traditions.

Extremely wise, but (therefore?) always silent.

In other traditions Freyja is Óðinn's wife, and a third tradition claims that Frigg and Freyja are one and the same.

In English Friday is named after Frigg, in Scandinavia Friday (*"Fredag"*) is named after Freyja.

HEIMDALLR

A vicious warrior, and a steadfast guard of Ásgarðr. He is keeping an eye on the bridge Bifröst without pauses, and will blow his enormous horn – Gjallarhorn – when enemies approach.

LOKI

His origin is in Útgarðar, and he is a jǫtunn that became friends with Óðinn and Þórr.

He even tricked another jǫtunn to build a great protective wall around Ásgarðr, for free.

Loki is sometimes called *"The Trickster God"*, as he is somewhat a conundrum.

Just like Óðinn – but even more so – he has an agenda of his own, but where Óðinn's purpose is to gain wisdom at all costs, and gather skilled warriors for Valhǫll and the last struggle, Loki's aim is more unclear. It seems like he's determined to make things more interesting, at all costs.

Or, as you say in English: *"Just for the hell of it"*.

Loki is indispensable as he is the one who sets things in motion, even Ragnarǫk, and without him there wouldn't be as many good stories about the Æsir.

It is impossible to love Loki, just like it is impossible to hate him.

Loki is the epitome of ADHD: He will work tirelessly to do good, but when he is bored, he will incite chaos and mayhem.

Loki is the one who you will fear but respect, and who will make you laugh.

MÍMIR

Mímir is the keeper of the well of wisdom.

After the great war between the Æsir and Vanir Mímir was beheaded, and the head was sent to the Æsir. Óðinn smeared the head with magical herbs, thus keeping the head alive, where it now stands in his chambers as an advisor.

IÐUNN

Iðunn is keeping the magical apples that provide the Æsir with eternal youth and life.

NJÖRÐR

Njörðr is a Vanir, but lives in Ásgarðr.

Along with his children, Freyja and Freyr, he moved there in a hostage exchange to end the war between Æsir and Vanir.

Njörðr is a áss for the weather, the sea, fishermen and sailing merchants.

SKAÐI

Skaði is a jǫtunn princess who went to Ásgarðr to marry the most beautiful of all the Æsir men – Baldr.

She was only allowed to look at their feet when choosing, so by mistake she chose Njörðr, who lives by the sea, and stands with his feet in the water for much of the day.

He longed for the sea, and she longed for the mountains, and after a while they divorced.

Skaði now lives in the mountains where she is hunting with bow and arrow, and doesn't want to be disturbed.

GEFION

Gefion and Óðinn were talking to the human king of the Danes. He resided in the island of Funen, and in honour of Óðinn he named his Town Oðense.

Grateful for this, Óðinn wanted to give him more land.

Gefion visited the king of the Sveas (present day central Sweden), named Gylfe, and gave him a huge fortune in gold, in return for land.

He said she could have all the land she could carve out with a plough in a day and a night.

He didn't know she was a ásynja and with four magical oxen in front of a large plough she took so much land that she could create the island of Zealand, in Denmark.

The land she removed from the Svea kingdom was replaced by a lake; Mälaren, around the island of Birka (the capital of the Svea kingdom, close to present day Stockholm).

In other editions of the story the land she removes becomes the lakes Vättern and Vänern.

Gefion is a virgin, and will take care of all human women who die a virgin, in the afterlife.

BALDR

Baldr is a (natural) son of Óðinn.

Baldr is good. He is wise, bright, beautiful, and nobody can say a bad word about him.

The Æsir all agree that as long as they have Baldr everything's going to be okay.

To keep him safe his mother (Frigg or Freyja) makes an agreement with everything in the world not to harm Baldr.

"Everything?" Asks Loki.

And she admits not to have an agreement with mistletoe, since it is also associated with love and beauty.

When the Æsir tests Baldr's immortality, by shooting arrows at him, Loki makes an arrow of mistletoe, and tricks the blind Höder to shoot it at Baldr.

Baldr dies, and this is the beginning of Ragnarǫk.

NEO-PAGANISM

In Scandinavia neo-paganism is the revival of the forn siðr (*"the old ways"*).

In other words it's the wish to relate to Óðinn, Þórr, Freyr, etc., and the might of nature. Mind you: Not *"believe in"*, but *"relate to"*! There's a huge difference there.

It is possible to think of the Æsir and Vanir as supernatural beings, but at least just as common to view them symbolically or as metaphors of some sort.

It's practised in many different ways, but emphasis is often on modern priorities, like nature preservation, women's rights (as opposed to Christianity, Islam and Hinduism), and personal freedom.

Obviously the forces of nature have been very important in the bronze age and iron age, but more in relation to producing crops than preserving the integrity of nature, so there's one update.

Another update is the idea that Æsir and Vanir hold moral virtues, which wasn't necessarily the perception a thousand years ago.

Women's rights were not an issue in the iron age, and it was a very patriarchal society, but women had positions and were respected much more than in the mediaeval Christian society that followed, so it is also a reformulation and update.

From sagas and archaeological finds practitioners try to establish rites as close to how they may have been performed a thousand years ago, and that's the hard bit, as descriptions of rites are extremely sparse (as in: Non existent).

In Scandinavia some pagan rituals and beliefs have never been eradicated by Christianity, for the simple reason that the monotheistic religions have nothing to bring to the table in relation to practical issues like farming and human relations.

The Bible and Qur'an don't tell me when to sow and when to harvest, how to treat an infection or deal with infertility.

On the contrary, early Christianity fought to replace medicine, the tools of nature, counselling and open minded approaches with piety and prayer.

Neo-paganism, just like most other kinds of modern spirituality and *"new age"* can be observed as countering religious establishments that can't accommodate modernity, science and globalisation.

The thinking is that *"book-religions"* was a temporary influence that didn't stand the test of time.

For *"In nyí siðr"* (*"the new way"* – Christianity) it was obviously hugely beneficial to have a written guideline, and the inter-european uniformity it created, but it was also its downfall, as the Bible isn't updated as regularly as is necessary to prevail.

The success of Christianity, in the ancient Roman Empire, as well as in mediaeval Scandinavia, was obviously the moral guidance towards social equality, especially in relation to the afterlife, where a firm believer could enter the heavenly kingdom without valuable grave goods and the funds to pay for an expensive funeral ritual.

These benefits have been integrated in the *"new-old-ways"*; neo-paganism.

Meanwhile the Lutheran church in Scandinavian countries are trying desperately to catch up, with rainbow flags to signal inclusion, in spite of the claim that they are based on the Bible. Hm... The Bible clearly states that homosexual men should be stoned to death.

It's like making a machine with a manual, updating the machine, but not the manual. It creates confusion.

Imagine Jesus saying *"You have been using the same book for 1,500 years? Are you fucking kidding me.???"*

It's maybe hard to imagine Jesus saying that.

So much easier to imagine Óðinn being so straight forward.

And that just might be the appeal of neo-paganism.

You can read more at asa-community.se and fornsidr.dk.

CHRISTIAN MYTHOLOGY, HISTORY AND PRACTISE

Christianity came into existence around 50 BC, as an offspring from the monotheistic Jewish faith, during the Roman Empire's occupation of Palestine, actually as a rebellion against religious authorities – but oddly enough not against the Romans.

Around 80 years later nailed to a carpenter named Jesus, though he is presumably a composite character, like so many others in the oral tradition.

According to the mythology his birth was given a lot of attention, after which nothing happened for about 30 years, until he revealed himself publicly to be the son of God, speaking out against religious leaders, and holding magic powers.

This *"blasphemy"* led the religious authorities to request the Romans to execute him.

So he was, but in vain, as he managed to rise from the grave, and give some final guidance to his followers, before ascending to heaven.

The following years his doctrine gained a rising number of followers, and his life story was described, in parts or entirety, in about 40 so-called *"gospels"*.

As mentioned Christianity was a promise to poor people about afterlife salvation, which in older religions was a luxury reserved for the rich and free (non-slaves).

This made Christianity highly popular, and in spite of extremely violent persecution the number of followers kept rising.

Jesus Christ was in fact the second most important person in Christianity, as the real main character is Saint Peter, who managed to negotiate the ultra complex political, social and religious climate in the crumbling Roman Empire, and gain a landslide of followers, in spite of the persecution from more conservative powers.

It happened more or less simultaneously with the Roman Empire being divided into the Western and Eastern part, and the following decline of the Western part.

In c. 330 the East Roman – Byzantine – Emperor Constantine held a Council where parts of the Jewish Scriptures and 4 out of the 40 stories about Jesus were collected and edited, for the creation of the Bible.

This streamlined Christianity somewhat, as there were contradictory perceptions of Jesus' divinity, actions and words, both in congregations and scriptures.

The Byzantine Empire became officially Christian, and from Constantinople Christianity spread like wildfire in all directions.

A division arose, and two editions came to dominate Eastern and Western Europe, respectively. From Constantinople the Orthodox Christianity, and from Rome the Catholic Christianity, but the message was basically the same: Through prayer, piety and submission to God – who is also Jesus – everybody can achieve a seat in Heaven.

The Patriarch in the Orthodox Church and the Pope in the Catholic church became immensely powerful, and through their deputies (bishops) their influence undermined the regency of all European kingdoms.

The outcome was uniformity in Europe, and gave rise to rather large empires.

Unfortunately it also punished all hesitation towards the church doctrine and power ruthlessly, all the way from kings and rulers to the local Völve fixing flesh wounds with herbs.

The Christian doctrine teaches humility towards God (and religious authorities), abolition of all other deities, and prayer as the only means to solve problems – whether political, moral, mental or physical.

Increasingly people started seeing everything as a part of God's divine plan, and all challenges as a punishment for sins.

Sins in the Christian terminology is insubordination towards God's plan.

Sex before marriage, women handling holy scriptures, medical treatment, disobedience towards political and religious authorities and many other things were on the list of *"sins"* in the mediaeval Christian church.

In Scandinavia Christianity came as a slightly watered down edition.

Around 850 the Danish king Hrorikr gave the missionary Ansgar permission to build churches in the trading settlements of Heiðabýr and Ribe, but the first signs of Christianity might have been as early as 150 years before that.

The last known blót festival was in Sweden around 1350.

That's 650 years of transition.

In the transition period many mixed the faiths and traditions, and these mixes are still visible in Scandinavia.

No doubt some Vikings saw *"Inn Nýi siðr"* (*"the new ways"* – Christianity) and *"Hvítakristr"* (*"White Christ"*) as something appealing, exciting and exotic, in much the same way some Europeans see certain Asian religions now.

For many Vikings – especially people of power – the conversion to Christianity was a tactical or political move, more than actually changing faith – and an easy one too: The faith they claimed to leave had no authorities or punishment for leaving.

Obviously they didn't have the same craving for change, as many others on the continent, since the Forn Siðr was less oppressive and egalitarian than pagan religions in southern Europe.

In the 1530s Scandinavia was reformed to the Lutheran church, and parted with the Catholic Church in Rome.

The general ideology within modern Christianity is that as long as you are humble before God and ask for forgiveness, you can get away with almost anything.

After two world wars Christianity only remains as a cultural phenomenon, sharing space with pagan traditions equally, in Scandinavia.

Now, in Scandinavia, Easter is celebrated as days off, midsummer solstice is celebrated as a heathen festival, and on December 24th we celebrate Jul, which has become a mixed Christian-pagan celebration. In the evening we will eat an unhealthy meal of roast pork and the children will open presents. The house is decorated with Nisser, fir and fruit.

About half of all children are baptised in the church, mainly for traditional reasons, just like 30 percent of all marriages are blessed in the church, and almost all burials take place in the church.

There hasn't been put a lot of energy put into creating alternatives to church burials, but more and more people become aware of other options.

That almost sums up our entire relationship with the church.

All the Scandinavian national churches are Lutheran, but there are visible signs of influence from east and west. In Sweden the church is open all day, and people can walk in from the street and light candles. Even the architecture of many Swedish churches have hints to the Orthodox traditions from Kievan Rus. In Denmark and Norway the influence is visibly more western, and the churches are closed, when there's no service going on.

In Norway it's still possible to find the wooden stave church-es that are built in the traditional architecture of pagan temples.

JEWS IN THE IRON AGE

As Muslim empires grew in the late 700s, simultaneously with Christian kingdoms, Jews became a very important group of go-betweens.

Firstly they had no part in the conflict of interests, secondly they had no rules about handling money, which is somewhat problematic in Islam, as fees and interest are illegal (*"haram"*).

So they got the role of being bankers, couriers and diplomatic envoys.

This, in turn, made some Jews incredibly rich, well travelled and well informed.

For the Abbasid caliphate and Al-Andalus the Jews were absolutely indispensable.

It's worth remembering that Jews are not just a religious group, but even an ethnic group, that c. 500 years previously was driven out of their country, and at this point had no ambitions of returning.

The anti-jewish sentiments were still a few hundred years into the future.

Jewish merchants are known to have visited Heiðabýr, and later Schleswig, on numerous occasions, and have also made the acquaintance of Vikings in Al-Andalus.

Ibrahim Ibn Yacoub Al-Tartushi, who visited the Vikings in southern Denmark on behalf of Al-Andalus, was actually Jewish.

SERKLAND – THE MUSLIMS IN HISTORIC VIKING AGE

Islam was the new kid on the block, but an extremely fast growing kid.

In the prophet Muhammad's own lifetime vast areas came under Muslim control, and after his death in 632 AD Muslim caliphates spread throughout the map in the Arab peninsula, the middle east, north Africa, and present day Spain.

Islam is a Christian sect, in many ways, giving the same promise of a place in heaven, even for the poor and the slaves.

Islam puts emphasis on strict rules about all sorts of behaviour, how to dress, when to pray, what to eat, and hygiene. None of these rules are in conflict with Christianity, as such, and for a short while there was peaceful coexistence.

In fact many people in the Middle East converted to Islam, as it was in many ways more *"chill"* than mediaeval Christianity, that had even more rules, harder misogyny, and several long periods of fasting.

What made Christians and Muslims cross swords was territorial ambitions.

This became the primary occupation for the Varangian Guard in the Byzantine empire, and it also became the end of the Varangian Guard, when Constantinople fell to the Muslim Ottomans in 1453.

Kievan Rus shared parts of its southern border with the Abbasid caliphate, and for a short period the Samanid empire, but there are no records of how that panned out.

Al-Andalus ended in Spain when it was conquered by Christians in 1492, and with that the religious tolerance. Pagans, Muslims and Jews were forcefully converted, driven out or killed, and from Spain a zero tolerance policy spread to the rest of Europe.

Even the Muslims who had voluntarily converted to Christianity were later driven out or killed.

The years of insane paranoia had begun, with the Spanish Inquisition, witch-hunts and the southbound crusades.

The Vikings didn't participate in these crusades to the *"Holy Land"*, but that definitely doesn't whitewash them; when they were christened a few hundred years earlier the Vikings actually invented crusades.

ENCYCLOPEDIA

-datter

Daughter in Danish and Norwegian patronymes.

-dotter

Daughter in Swedish patronymes.

-dottír

Daughter in Icelandic patronymes.

-r

Added to a name or title to make it masculine. Like "Gormr". Or "MacBookr"...

-sen

Son in Danish and Norwegian patronymes.

-sson

Son in Swedish and Icelandic patronymes.

Abbasid Caliphate

All of the Arabian peninsula, northern Egypt, Iraq and southern Turkey 750–1258 and 1261–1517.

Adam of Bremen

1040–1081

A Christian cleric travelling in Scandinavia, describing the lifestyle and religion, as a guest at King Svend Estridsen's court. Many of his descriptions are based on hearsay, from priests and missionaries, and much is pure fiction.

Ahmad Ibn Fadlan

879–960

A Baghdad (Abbasid Caliphate) envoy to the Volga area, where he described the Rus Vikings he met, with a wonderful mix of fascination and horror.

Al-Andalus

711-1492 the Islamic state covering the Iberian peninsula (present day Spain and Portugal).

Álfheimr

Home of the Ljósálfar (Light Elves).

Alþing

Parliament. Also see Þing.

Anders Lundt Hansen

Historian, author and lecturer. One of Denmark's leading experts on Iron Age and medieval Scandinavia.

Angrboða

A jǫtunn woman, and temporary mate of Loki. With Loki she mothers the Fenrisúlfr, Hel and Jǫrmungandr.

Annales Bertiniani

Annals of Saint Bertin. Practical annual reports of raids carried out by various Viking groups from Scandinavia in the Frankish areas, plundered Carolingian monasteries and episcopal cities 830-882.

Asatro/Asetro/Æsirtrú

The modern Scandinavian word for the Norse religion; Forn Siðr.

Ásbrú

The Æsir's bridge. Another name for Bifröst.

Ásgarðr

The land of the Æsir, and location for Valhǫll and Fólkvangr (et al). Literally Æsir + Gård.

Askr & Embla

The first two humans.

Ásynja

Female deity

Babylon

Ancient city located on the lower Euphrates river in present day Iraq. In the Iron Age the capital of the Abbasid Caliphate and an important trading destination for the Varangian/Rus Vikings. The city declined in the 1200s.

Baghdad

Capital of Iraq and the second-largest city in the Arab world after Cairo. Like Babylon important trading destination for the Varangian/Rus Vikings.

Baldr

Baldr is a (natural) son of Óðinn.
Baldr is good. He is wise, bright, beautiful, and nobody can say a bad word about him. When Baldr dies Ragnarǫk begins.

Beowolf

"Old English epic poem consisting of 3,182 alliterative lines. It is one of the most important and most often translated works of Old English literature. The only certain dating is for the manuscript, which was produced between 975 and 1025.
The story is set in pagan Scandinavia in the 6th century. Beowulf, a hero of the Gautar, comes to the aid of Hrothgar, the king of the Danes, whose mead hall in Heorot has been under attack by the monster Grendel. After Beowulf slays him, Grendel's mother attacks the hall and is then

defeated. Victorious, Beowulf goes home to Gautarland and becomes king of the Gautar.

Fifty years later, Beowulf defeats a dragon, but is mortally wounded in the battle.

After his death, his attendants cremate his body and erect a barrow on a headland in his memory.

Berserkir

Berserker. It likely means "bear-shirt", "someone who wears a coat made out of a bear's skin" or attack more or less naked. Known to induce fear by being furiously violent and out of control. Most likely they have functioned more like cheerleaders than actually made a practical impact in the battlefield.

Bifröst

The magical and invisible bridge that connects the different worlds in Yggdrasil, like Ásgarðr, Jǫtunheimr and Miðgarðr. Only the Æsir can use the bridge. It becomes vaguely visible when sun follows rain (as the rainbow).

Birka

Birka, on the island of Björkö in present-day Sweden, was an important Iron Age trading centre which handled goods from Scandinavia as well as many parts of the European continent and the Orient. Björkö is located in Lake Mälaren, 30 kilometres west of Stockholm.

Bjarni Herjólfsson

?–?

Merchant captain, based in Norway, but visiting his father every summer in Iceland. In 986 he arrived in Iceland only to learn his father had gone to Greenland with Eiríkur "Rauði" Þorvaldsson. In an attempt to reach Greenland he was blown off course, and landed on the Canadian coast, present day Gulf of Saint Lawrence in Canada. He didn't stay to explore the lands, but reported when he arrived in Greenland, where Leifur Eiríksson and his sister Freydís Eiríksdóttir chose to compile a colonising expedition 14 years later. It is unknown how many expeditions have been carried out before the settlement in year 1000.

Björn Járnsíða

There are conflicting stories about his origin, as he is mentioned as the king of both areas in Sweden and Denmark. Some vague mentions of raiding in the river seine, but the story gets more precise when his adventures in the Mediterranean are described. He came with 60 ships and raided his way along the coasts of Al Andalus, southern France, Sicily and north Africa. Battles and hard weather made him return to Frankia with only 20 ships.

Blood Eagle

According to some stories it is the execution method of cutting through the skin and the flesh along the spine with a knife, separating the ribs from the spine with an axe, draw the ribcage apart, and spread out the lungs to resemble eagle wings, while the person is still alive. This is disputed, as other sources claim that blood eagle simply means leaving the dead face down on the battlefield, and let the scavenger birds eat through the back.

Blót

Sacrifice or worship.

Blótgydje

Another word for Völve.

Borre

Important Iron Age location in Norway.

Brattahlíð

The farm and trading station built by Eiríkur "Rauði" Þorvaldsson (Erik the Red) in Greenland.

Brísingamen

The magical necklace that makes Freyja irresistible to everyone. It is forged by four black elves and she had to spend a night with each one of them to buy the necklace.

Byzans

Another name for Constantinople/Miklagarðr. Present day Istanbul.

Byzantine Empire

Also referred to as the Eastern Roman Empire, the continuation of the Roman Empire primarily in its eastern provinces during Late Antiquity and the Middle Ages, when its capital city was Constantinople.

It survived the fall of the Western Roman Empire in the 5th century AD and continued to exist until the fall of Constantinople to the Ottoman Empire in 1453. During most of its existence, the empire remained the most powerful economic, cultural, and military force in the Mediterranean world. Its citizens continued to refer to their empire as the Roman Empire and to themselves as Romans.

At its height it consisted of present day southern Italy, Bulgaria, Croatia, North Macedonia, Greece, Turkey, Israel, Palestine, and northern Egypt. Vikings never conquered the capital Miklagarðr (old Norse name for Constantinople), but managed to besiege it so successfully that favour-

able trade agreements were made, and the emperor later formed the famous Varangian Guard (see that).
Kievan Rus (see that) exported fur, amber, steel and especially slaves in large quantities to the Byzantine Empire."

Carl Emil Doepler

1824–1905
Scenographer, created horned helmets for the first Bayreuther Festival production of Wagner's "Der Ring des Nibelungen", in 1876, and thereby starting the popular myth that Viking warriors wore horned helmets.

Carolingian

Another name for the Holy Roman Empire.

Cat Jarman

Norwegian/English bio archaeologist and writer specialising in Vikings. Senior Adviser on academic content development for the new Museum of the Viking Age, University of Oslo.

Danegæld

"Protection money", paying Danes to go away, in order not to be subject to a massacre.

Danelagen

The Danelaw, also known as the Danelagh.
The part of England in which the laws of the Danes held sway; about 80% of present day England and a small part of Scotland.
Confederacy under the Kingdom of Denmark from the invasion of the Great Heathen Army into England in the year 865 until 1002 – the St. Brice's Day massacre of the Danes (see that).

Danes

The Iron Age people in Denmark, Norway and southern Sweden.

Dannevirke

30 km long defence line in southern Jutland, at an old border between Denmark and the Holy Roman Empire. The largest part is 3 km long, 3 metres wide and 3 metres tall; made of 20 million stones.
Most of the defence line was built of earthen embankments with wooden palisades.

Dublin

The capital of Ireland, established as an important Viking slave trading centre during the Iron Age, though inhabited since the Stone Age.

Dvergr

Dwarfs. Another name for Svartálfr (black elves).

Dökkálfar

Dark Elves. Another name for Svartálfr.

Einherjar

Those who have died in battle and are brought to Fólkvangr or Valhǫll by Valkyrja.

Eiríkur "Rauði" Þorvaldsson

950–1003

Erik "the Red" Thorvaldsson. Discovered and settled in southern Greenland. Father to Leifur "Heppni" Eiríksson and Freydís Eiríksdóttir. The nickname "Rauði" (Red) is unexplained, but could refer to hair colour or temper.

Eric of Pomerania

1382–1459

Nephew to Margrete Valdemarsdatter, officially king of all Scandinavian countries 1389–1442, while all decisions were made by his aunt until her death in 1412. After coup d'états in all the countries in 1439, he settled in Visby castle in Gotland, from where he engaged in piracy. From 1449 to 1459 he ruled as the count of Pomerania. Perhaps King Erik's most far-ranging act was the introduction of the Sound Dues (Øresundtolden) in 1429, which was to last until 1857. It consisted of the payment of sound dues by all ships wishing to enter or exit the Baltic Sea from the Atlantic.

Erik the Red

See Eiríkur "Rauði" Þorvaldsson

Eske Willerslev

Danish evolutionary geneticist notable for his pioneering work in molecular anthropology, palaeontology, and ecology at University of Cambridge. In short: This dude knows everything about DNA! (His twin brother Rane Willerslev is Director of the National Museum of Denmark)

Fenrisúlfr

The Fenris Wolf – a monstrosity of a mythological wolf.

Fimbulvintr

Fimbulvintr is the harsh winter that precedes the end of the world – Ragnarǫk – and ends all life on Earth.
In 536 AD two major volcanic eruptions created a global period of cooling, often referred to as "three years without summer". The global death toll was enormous, and the

event is now thought to be the origin of the myth of Fimbulvintr. Also read about Ragnarǫk.

Flóki Vilgerðarson

?–?

"Hrafna"-Flóki Vilgerðarson. According to saga he named Iceland. Leading of the first attempt to populate Iceland, and failed.

Fólkvangr

Freyja's estate in Ásgarðr, where she keeps, feeds, and train the best Einherjar for the final battle at Ragnarǫk.

Forn Siðr

"Old Ways". A description of Norse paganism, that didn't have a name, as opposed to ""Inn Nyí Siðr"" (the new ways – Christianity).
Also see "Neo-Paganism"."

Fornyrðislag

"Old story metre". The Norse poets tended to break up their verses into stanzas of from two to eight lines (or more).
The Norse poets tended to make each line a complete syntactic unit.

Frankish annals

Also known as the Annales Laurissenses Maiores ('Greater Lorsch Annals'), a series of annals composed in Latin in the Carolingian Frankia, recording year-by-year the state of the monarchy from 741 to 829.

Freydís Eiríksdóttir

965–?

Daughter of Eiríkur "Rauði" Þorvaldsson, sister to Leifur "Heppni" Eiríksson, among the first settlers in Vinland.

Freyja

"Love, death and magic are the main areas of interest for this beautiful young and endlessly attractive Æsir.
Or is she?
The Svartálfr made her the magical necklace Brísingamen that will make everyone see her as irresistibly desirable.
She resides in Fólkvangr, where she is responsible for the Valkyrja. She has first choice of Einherjar, before Óðinn gets the second half. Freyja is Vanir, daughter of Njörðr and sister to Freyr. In Scandinavia Friday ("Fredag") is named after Freyja."

Freyr

Vanir, son of Njörðr, brother to Freyja, and when they came to Ásgarðr the siblings were married. As sibling marriage is common among Vanir, but prohibited to Æsir, they were forced to divorce.

Frigg

"Óðinn's wife, according to some traditions.
Extremely wise, but (therefore?) always silent.
In other traditions Freyja is Óðinn's wife, and a third tradition claims that Frigg and Freyja are one and the same.
In English Friday is named after Frigg.

Garðaríki

Old Norse name for Kievan Rus (see that).

Garðr

Farm, Estate or even Land.

Gautar

A large North Germanic tribe who inhabited Götaland ("land of the Gautars") in present day southern Sweden from antiquity until the late Middle Ages.

Gefion

A virgin Æsir, and will take care of all human women who die a virgin, in the afterlife.

Geri & Freki

Óðinn's two wolves.

Gimlé

Gimlé is a place where the heroes of Ragnarök are foretold to live. The most beautiful place in Ásgarðr, more beautiful than the sun.

Gjallarhorn

Heimdallr's horn that will sound when jǫtunn approach Ásgarðr.

Godo Friduf, Godfred rex Danorum

In 804 the Danish king, according to the Frankish Annals.

Gormr "Gamli" Hardeknudsson

C. 895-960

Gorm the old, first ruler of all of Denmark(?). Ruled from Jelling, where he made the first of the Jelling runestones in honour of his wife Þórvi. Father of Haraldr "Blátǫnn" Gormsson.

Gotar

A North Germanic tribe inhabiting the island of Gotland.

Gungner

Óðinn's spear.

Gustav Eriksson "Vasa"

1496–1560
1523–1560 king of Sweden, and the creator of sovereign
Sweden, effectively ending the Kalmar Union.
Born a nobility he led the independence war against the
Danish king Kristian II "Tyrant".
His family ruled Sweden until 1654.

Gård

See "Garðr".

Harald Bluetooth

See Haraldr "Blátonn" Gormsson

Harald Finehair

See Haraldr Hárfagri

Harald Hårderåde

See Haraldr "harðráði" Sigurðarson.

Haraldr "Blátonn" Gormsson

958–986
In popular culture know as Harald Bluetooth. Haraldr
Gormsson, nicknamed "Blátonn" (literally "Blue tooth").
Presumably because of a tooth with a dead nerve.
According to himself the creator of the Danish Kingdom,
including Norway, and declaring all of Denmark Christian.

A digital technology, invented in Sweden, carries the name Bluetooth, in his honour, and the runes for B and T combined in the logo. Yes, you may look at your phone now. A new theory states that his nickname – in his honour or to mock him – was actually "Blótan" ("giving offerings" or "worshipping").

Haraldr "harðráði" Sigurðarson

1015–1066

King of Norway, and known in English history as "the last Viking", as he was killed in the Battle of Stamford Bridge, which concludes the Viking Age in England, September 25th 1066. Also known as Harald Hårderåde.

Haraldr Hárfagri

850–932

In English known as Harald Fairhair or Harald Finehair. The first king of an independent and unified Norway. He is mentioned in Hrafnsmál, Glymdrápa, Sendibitr, Íslendingabók, Skarðsárbók, Ágrip af Nóregskonungasögum, Historia Norwegiæ, Fagrskinna, Heimskringla, Egil's Saga, Grettis saga, Ragnarssona þáttr, Flóamanna saga, Vatnsdæla saga, Orkneyinga saga AND Flateyjarbók, but there are nevertheless reasons to believe that Norway was neither independent nor united in his lifetime. This is public relations and fake news on a level of its own. Haraldr was married three times, to Ragnhild "inn Rika" Eiríksdóttir, Åsa Håkonsdotter and Snøfrid Svåsedottir, but we don't know if it was one at a time or polygamy.

Hávamál

(The Tall One's speech) is a quatrain in the older Edda. The quatrain is a long didactic poem about what is considered good and bad behaviour, with Óðinn using his own life to exemplify. Humility, hospitality, loyalty and gratitude are urged.

Heiðabýr

Important Iron Age Viking trading city in southern Denmark (now in Germany).
Raided and burned in 1049 by Haraldr "Harðráði" Sigurðarson (Harald Hårderåde).

Heimdallr

A vicious warrior, and a steadfast guard of Ásgarðr. He is keeping an eye on the bridge Bifröst without pauses, and will blow his enormous horn – Gjallerhorn – when enemies approach.

Hel

One of the three children by Loki and Angrboða (the two others are the wolf Fenris and the Miðgarðr snake). This deity was banished to the realm of the dead, Helheimr, in Niflheimr. "Hel" can also be short for Helheimr.

Helga of Kyiv

890–969

Mainly known as Olga of Kyiv, married to Ingvarr Hrøríkʀsson and mother of Sveinald Ingvarrsson. After the murder of her husband Ingvarr in 945 she ruled on behalf of her son until 960. In 950 she visited Miklagarðr (Constantinople) and converted to Orthodox Christianity. In order to preserve stability in Kievan Rus, revenge the death of her husband, and convert the population to Christianity she has countless lives on her conscience, and yet she is today the official saint of both Russia and Ukraine. If you were looking for a shield-maiden, she's the one!

Helgi the Wise

?-940

Son of Hrøríkr (Rurik), married to Helga and father of
Valdamarr Sveinaldsson. Better known as Igor of Kiev
or Igor Rurikovich. Ingvarr twice besieged Miklagarðr
(Constantinople), in 941 and 944, and although Greek fire
destroyed part of his fleet, he concluded a favourable treaty
with the Byzantine Emperor Constantine VII in 945.
Ingvarr was killed while collecting tax from the Drevlians
in 945.

Helheimr

Often just referred to as "Hel". The realm of the dead.
A dull place with not much going on. Not to be confused
with Hell, where the dead are punished for eternity – that's
a different religion.

Helluland

"Land of Flat Rocks". Baffin Island in present day Canada.

Henbane

Toxic plant, in small doses a hallucinogen.

Hil

Hail! (And, yes, unfortunately, that became the German
"Heil").

Hildisvíni

Freyja's magical boar she rides into battle.

Hird

A group of warriors

Hnefatafl

Viking age board game, sometimes referred to as "Viking Chess".

Hǫðr

Óðinn's blind son. Loki tricks him into killing Baldr, thus starting Ragnarǫk.

Holm

Island in an urban environment. Known from e.g. Stockholm. Most islands in Scandinavian cities are named Holm-something. Manhattan is actually a Holm, just like Hong Kong Island…

Holmganga

A duel in a confined space (see "Holm"). At least in theory, anyone offended could challenge the other party to holmganga regardless of their differences in social status. This could be a matter of honour, ownership or property, demand of restitution of debt or legal disagreement.

Holmgarðr

The first major Viking city in the Rus empire. Today known as Novgorod (or Velikij Novgorod), in Russia. The actual site was present day Rurikovo Gorodische, 2 km south of the current city. Established by Hrøríkr (Rurik).

Holy Roman Empire

Stretching from central Italy to the Danish border, and from eastern France into the middle of Poland (speaking in present day countries), an empire created by Charlemagne (or Charles the Great).

Hrólfr

870–928

Göngu-Hrólfr, Rolf the Walker or Rollo. Hrólfr and other Viking warlords were wearing down the Holy Roman Empire by attacking cities and monasteries in the river Seine. The emperor struck a deal with him in 911: By giving him the northern part of the country to rule, as Count of Rouen, he would also become a buffer-state and protect the rest of the empire from further Viking raids. This became Normandy. Rollo's son and heir, William Longsword, and grandchild, Richard the Fearless, forged the Duchy of Normandy into West Frankia's most cohesive and formidable principality. Hrólfr is the great-great-great-grandfather of William the Conqueror, who won the Battle of Hastings and became the progenitor of the House of Normandy in England. The Göngu (Walker) nickname is, according to legend, because he was so big no horse could carry him.

Hrøríkr

?–879

Commonly known as Rurik, founder of the first Rus Empire in eastern Europe, as he established himself in Holmgarðr (Novgorod) in 862. Hrøríkr has been considered the founder of the Rurik dynasty, which went on to rule Kievan Rus' and its principalities, and ultimately the Tsardom of Russia. Vasili IV, who reigned until 1610, was the last Rurikid monarch of Russia.

Hugin & Munin

Two ravens belonging to Óðinn. Means "Thought" and "Memory". They are in effect his secret service.

Hvide Krist

See Hvítakristr.

Hvítakristr

"White Christ". The Iron Age Viking's name for Jesus Christ. Probably because new converts were obligated to wear white clothes a week after being baptised, but we don't know for sure.

Iðunn

Iðunn is keeping the magical apples that provide the Æsir with almost eternal youth and life.

Igor of Kiev

See Ingvarr Hrøríkrsson

Ingvarr the far travelled

See Yngvarr Víðförli

Ingvarr Hrøríkrsson

875–945

Son of Hrøríkr (Rurik), married to Helga and father of Valdamarr Sveinaldsson. Better known as Igor of Kiev or Igor Rurikovich. Ingvarr twice besieged Miklagarðr (Constantinople), in 941 and 944, and although Greek fire destroyed part of his fleet, he concluded a favourable treaty with the Byzantine Emperor Constantine VII in 945. Ingvarr was killed while collecting tax from the Drevlians in 945.

Inn Nyí Siðr

"The new way" – Christianity.

Ivar the Boneless

See Ívarr "Hinn Beinlausi" Ragnarsson

Ívarr "Hinn Beinlausi" Ragnarsson

?–873

According to sagas son of Ragnarr Loðbrók, and the leader of the Great Heathen Army in 865. Known as Ímar king of Dublin between 870-873. "Bein" in old Norse can mean bone, 'boner' or legs, and we have no idea if he had a bone disease, was missing a leg or two, or he was impotent. A fourth theory suggests that "Boneless" meant extremely flexible.

Jarl

Earl

Jelling

Old and important historical town in the history of Denmark. In the Iron Age it served as the royal seat of the first Monarchs of the Kingdom of Denmark. Jelling is the site of a large stone ship and two large burial mounds, as well as the Jelling runestones.

Jelling stones

Massive carved runestones from the 900s, in the town of Jelling in Denmark. The older of the two Jelling stones was raised by King Gormr "Gamli" Hardeknudsson in memory of his wife Þórvi. The larger of the two stones was raised by King Gormr's son, Haraldr "Blátǫnn" Gormsson, in memory of his parents, celebrating his conquest of Denmark and Norway, and his conversion of the Danes to Christianity.

Jim Lyngvild

Controversial Danish artist with special interest in interpreting Viking finds.

Jomsborg

Semi-legendary Iron Age Viking stronghold at the southern coast of the Baltic Sea (medieval Wendland, modern Pomerania), that existed between the 960s and 1043. Its inhabitants were known as Jomsvikings. Jomsborg's exact location, or its existence, has not yet been established, though it is often maintained that Jomsborg was located on the eastern outlet of the Oder river, in Poland. Jomsvikings are legendary "warrior monk" mercenaries, kept isolated from women and other distractions.

Jǫrð

The Earth, observed as a goddess.

Jǫrmungandr

The Miðgarðr snake. A huge snake circumventing Miðgarðr, the human world. If Jǫrmungandr moves the world – or the ocean – will shake and move. Basically the explanation for ocean storms, oversize waves and earthquakes.

Jórvik

York. Most important city in Danelagen (see that).

Jǫtunheimr

Land of the Jǫtunn, where you find their fortress Útgarðar.

Jǫtunn

A group of giant monsters in the Norse religion, today used in Swedish (jätte) as "much", "large" or "a lot". Actually related to the Æsir, somehow.

Jul

In English sometimes spelled "Yule". Heathen celebration of the winter solstice, with very fluctuating dates, guided by the moon calendar.

When the Vikings became (somewhat) Christian the date became fixed on December 24th/25th, as it merged with the Christian Christmas celebration.

The word – and many traditions – are still used in Scandinavia.

Jætte/Jätte

See "Jǫtunn"

Kaupang

Important Norwegian Viking city. Founded in the 780s and abandoned for unknown reasons in the early 10th century.

Kiev

Also known as Kiev or Kijev.

The capital city of the Kievan Rus empire, in the Iron Age and mediaeval times.

Presently the capital of Ukraine.

Kievan Rus

The Rus empire in parts of present day Estonia, Russia, Ukraine, Belarus and Balkan.

Knud den store

See Knútr "Ínn ríki" Sveinsson

Knútr "Ínn ríki" Sveinsson

990–1035

In Danish Knud den store, in English Cnut the Great or Canute the Great. King of England from 1016, King of

Denmark from 1018, and King of Norway from 1028 until his death. The three kingdoms united under his rule are referred to as the North Sea Empire.

Kænugarðr

Old Norse alternative name for Kyiv (see that).

Lagerþa

?–?

A mythical female ruler and shield-maiden from Saxo Grammaticus "Chronicle of the Danes". Presumably inspired by the Norse deity Thorgerd.

Laila Kitzler Åhfeldt

Researcher, Riksantikvarieämbetet in Stockholm, who has developed a method to identify stonemasons of runestones.

Leif the Lucky

See Leifur "Heppni" Eiríksson

Leifur "Heppni" Eiríksson

Leif "The Lucky" Eriksson, son of Eiríkur "Rauði" Þorvaldsson. First settler in Vinland. The nickname can even be translated to "the Fortunate" or "the Happy".

Lejre

Today a small town in Denmark, close to Roskilde. Lejre's role in Danish history can be compared to that of Uppsala in Sweden. Lejre is sometimes assumed to have been the capital of a Iron Age kingdom sometimes referred to as the "Lejre Kingdom." According to early legends, it was ruled by kings of the Skjöldung dynasty, predecessors of the kings of medieval Denmark. Legends of the kings of Lejre are known from a number of medieval sources, including the twelfth-century Gesta Danorum written by Saxo Grammaticus.

Lisbeth Imer

Archaeologist and runolog at the National Museum of Denmark

Ljósálfar

The Light Elves, living in Álfheimr. Governed by the Æsir Freyr they make nature grow and thrive.

Lofoten

The first known town formation in northern Norway, and an important trading station for fishermen and whalers, and trade with the Sámi.

Loki

Loki is originally jǫtunn but becomes blood brother with Óðinn and lives in Ásgarðr. He is a multifaceted figure who does a lot of good, but also a lot of bad. He is often the one who sets the events in motion in the mythological stories.

Lund

From c. 990 the most important city in Scania, the Danish part of southern Sweden. Home to the first Scandinavian Archbishop. Lund Cathedral School (Katedralskolan) was founded in 1085 and is still active, as the oldest school in northern Europe.

Lögrétta

Supreme court.

Margrete Valdemarsdatter

1353–1412

Queen regnant of Denmark, Norway, and Sweden (including Finland, Iceland, Greenland, Shetland Islands and Faroe Islands) from the late 1380s until her death, and the founder of the Kalmar Union that joined the Scandinavian kingdoms together for over a century. Ruling on behalf of her nephew, she wasn't officially titled queen until many years after her death. The first official female ruler of Denmark was in fact Queen Margrethe the first, in 1972, but she chose the title "the second" in honour of Margrete Valdemarsdatter.

Margrethe Alexandrine Þórhildur Ingrid

1940–

Queen Margrethe ll of Denmark. In reign since 1972, as the first official female ruler (read about Margrete Valdemarsdatter!). In fact in direct bloodline from Knútr "Ínn ríki" Sveinsson (990-1035), and according to sagas from Ragnarr Loðbrók.

Mark

Old Norse: Forrest. Present day Scandinavian: Field or ground.

Markland

Viking location in Canada. Markland has been suggested to have been part of the Labrador coast. Lit. "Forrest Land".

Miðgarðr

Middle + gård, the middle earth; the human world. Where you are right now (I guess).

Miðgarðsormr

The Miðgarðr snake. See "Jǫrmungandr".

Miklagarðr

Constantinople, present day Istanbul.

Mímir

Mímir is the keeper of the well of wisdom; Mímisbrunnr. After the great war between the Æsir and Vanir Mimer was beheaded, and the head was send to the Æsir. Óðinn smeared the head with magical herbs, thus keeping the head alive, where it now stands in his chambers as an advisor. Óðinn gave one of his eyes to Mímir as payment to drink from the well of wisdom, or left his eye in the well to be able to see wisdom remotely.

Mímisbrunnr

Mímir's well of wisdom. See Mímir.

Mjölnír

Thor's magic hammer.

Móði & Magni

The sons of Þórr. Their names translate to "Wrath" and "Mighty," respectively.

Naddoðr

?–?

In the Sagas Naddoðr discovered Iceland, and named it Snow Island, before leaving for Faroe Islands, to settle there. Supposedly the grand father or great grand father of Þórvaldr Ásvaldsson, who is in turn father of Eiríkur "Rauði" Þorvaldsson.

Neo-paganism

In Scandinavia Neo-Paganism is the updated continuation of the Forn Siðr ("the old ways"). It is practiced in many different ways, but emphasis is often on conservation of history and traditions, healthy diet, respect for animals and nature, respects for the elders, focus on family, focus on women's rights (as opposed to Christianity, Islam and Hinduism), and hospitality. Often it can be seen as a mix of ancient world views with modern spirituality and respect for human rights and nature conservation.

Nīðing

Villain or "without honour". Often outlaw (Skóggangr or útlagi).

Niflheimr

The frozen world in the cosmology, in which the realm of the dead Helheimr also exists.

Nisse

A Nisse (Danish) or Tomte (Swedish) is a supernatural being that lives on every farm. They can be helpful or annoying, depending on how you treat them.
They are small, often described as about 40 cm, and the usual descriptions of their appearance has inspired the garden gnome.
They hide as best as they can, and hate to be spotted by humans.

Njörðr

"Njörðr is a Vanir, but lives in Ásgarðr.
Along with his children, Freyja and Freyr, he moved there in a hostage exchange to end the war between Æsir and Vanir.

Njörðr is a Æsir for the weather, the sea, fishermen and sailing merchants.

Norse Mythology

The Norse myths, legends and sagas, mainly about Æsir and Vanir.

North Sea Empire

The North Sea Empire, also known as the Anglo-Scandinavian Empire, was the personal union of the kingdoms of England, Denmark and Norway for most of the period between 1013 and 1042.

The first king to unite all three kingdoms was Sveinn ""tjúguskegg"" Haraldsson (Sweyn Forkbeard), king of Denmark since 986 and of Norway since 1000, when he conquered England in 1013.

He died in the following year, and his realm was divided. His son Knútr ""Ínn ríki"" Sveinsson (Cnut the Great) acquired England in 1016, Denmark in 1018 and Norway in 1028.

Novgorod

See "Holmgarðr".

Óðinn

Óðinn ("Odin", "Oden" or "Woden") is the main Æsir, according to most traditions.

He is somehow the originator of all the other Æsir, and therefore sometimes referred to as the "Allfather".

Other nicknames are "The Tall One" and "The One Eyed". Married to Frigg or Freyja, in different stories. Also read about Mímir, Frigg and Freyja.

Oleg the Wise

See Helgi the Wise

Olga of Kiev

See Helga of Kyiv

Ormr

The old Norse word for snake or serpent, both real and mythological. Mythologically it has in modern times been translated to dragon, not to be confused with winged fire spewing dragons in other mythologies. Mainly known from the "Miðgarðsormr" (the Miðgarðr snake).

Oslo

Norway's capital. According to the Norse sagas, Oslo was founded around 1049 by Haraldr Harðráði, but older burial mounts have been found.

ǫss

Alternative spelling for áss.

Pecheneg

A large group of tribes living around the Dnieper and Volga rivers, north of the Black Sea. Some of these tribes became part of the Kievan Rus empire, while others remained a thread to the empire.

Poetic Edda

Poetry collection depicting religious myths and fables. Written between 800 and 1000 in Norway and Iceland.

Poppo

?–?

Legendary missionary monk who carried a piece of glowing iron to prove the superiority of the Christian God to King Haraldr "Blátǫnn" Gormsson, according to sagas.

Prose Edda

Also known as "Snorri's Edda", one of the primary sources to knowledge about the Norse religion and myths, though written 200 years after the end of the (English) Viking Age, and in a Christian context.

Ragnarǫk

A foretold series of impending events, including a great battle in which numerous Æsir will perish (including Óðinn, Þórr Týr, Freyr, Heimdallr, and Loki); it will entail a catastrophic series of natural disasters, including the burning of the world, and culminate in the submersion of the world underwater. After these events, the world will rise again, cleansed and fertile, and the world will be repopulated by two human survivors, Líf and Lífþrasir.
Like a dawning the great hall Gimle will rise of the nothingness, and welcome all who has been good (Æsir, Vanir, humans etc.).
Ragnarǫk will follow the Fimbulvintr.

Ragnarr Loðbrók

?–?

Also known as Reginherus. A mythical character from "Ragnarr Loðbrók's saga" (et al), written sometime between 1200 and 1400 in Denmark. According to the saga he has five sons with his wife Áslaug: Ubbi, Sigurðr "Ormr í auga" Áslaugsson, Halfdan "Hvítserkr" Ragnarsson, Björn "Járnsíða" and Ívarr "hinn Beinlausi" Ragnarsson.

He is killed by the Northumberland king Ælla, by being thrown into a pit of snakes. According to the saga revenging his death was the reason for the formation of "the great heathen army". Loðbrók mean hairy trousers.

Ravnunge Tue

An important runestone master in Denmark. Has, among other things, carved the runes (and decorations) into four stones dealing with Þórvi, among them the two in Jelling.

Reykjavik

The capital of Iceland, established 870 AD, as the first Norse (and maybe human) settlement in Iceland. The name can be translated to "Steam Bay", and derives from the large number of natural hot springs.

Ribe

The first known – still existing – trade city in Denmark, close to the Danish-German border. Established around year 700. Primarily trade with England and Frisia. The seat of the first Christian church in Scandinavia.

Ring fortress

See "Trelleborg".

Rollo

See Hrólfr

Rorik

See Hrøríkr

Roskilde

City in Denmark, situated in the bottom of a fjord, west of present day Copenhagen. A number of Viking Ships were sunk in the Fjord to prevent attack. These ships are now in museum.

Rus

A group of Svea, Gotar and Gautar (see that) occupying parts of present day Estonia, Russia, Ukraine and Balkan. Sweden is today known as "Ruotsi" in Finnish, and "Root-si" in Estonian.

Samanid Empire

 A Persian Sunni Muslim empire in present day Persia and Central Asia, from 819 to 999

Sámi

The traditionally Sámi-speaking people inhabiting the region of Sápmi, which today encompasses large northern parts of Norway, Sweden, Finland, and of the Kola Peninsula in Russia.

The region of Sápmi was formerly known as Lapland, and the Sámi have historically been known as Lapps or Laplanders, but these terms are regarded as offensive by the Sámi.

Petroglyphs and archaeological findings related to the Sámi people, dating from about 10,000 BC can be found in the Scandinavian peninsula, close to and above the polar circle.

Saxo Grammaticus

1150–1220

Danish historian, theologian and author. Wrote the "Chronicle of the Danes" ("Gesta Danorum") for Bishop

Absalon of Lund and King Valdemar 1. His writings are glorifying the achievements of previous Danish rulers, and summarizes many myths and legends. His(?) character Amleth is without doubt the inspiration for Shakespeare's "Hamlet", and his(?) character Ragnarr Loðbrók became one of the leading characters in the History Channel/Netflix series "Vikings".

Seiðr

Magic and fortune-telling; the practice of seiðr is believed to be a form of magic which is related to both the telling and the shaping of the future. Practitioners are known to have been carrying a magical walking stick (which over time may have inspired to magic wands, as in Harry Potter), drums, and small engraved figures or dice.

Serkland

An old Norse name for the Islamic world.

Shield maiden

Female warrior. See "Skjoldmø".

Sigtuna

In the Iron Age a very important city in the Svea area by lake Mälaren.

Skaði

Skaði is a jǫtunn princess who went to Ásgarðr to marry the most beautiful of all the Æsir men – Baldr.
She was only allowed to look at their feet when choosing, so by mistake she chose Njörðr, who lives by the sea, and stands with his feet in the water for much of the day.
He longed for the sea, and she longed for the mountains, and after a while they divorced.

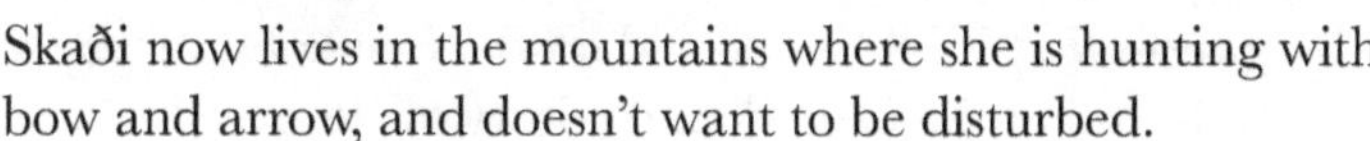

Skaði now lives in the mountains where she is hunting with bow and arrow, and doesn't want to be disturbed.

Skjald

Poet and/or storyteller, in some cases even singer. Also see Fornyrðislag.

Skjalðemjöð

Poetry booze – a drink that will inspire poetry.

Skjaldmær

Female warrior.

Skjǫld

The founder of Skjǫldungar, and the first king in Lejre, according to legend.

Skjoldmø

A female Viking warrior. Danish translation of skjaldmær.

Skjǫldungar

According to legends, a clan or dynasty of Danish kings, that in its time conquered and ruled Denmark and Sweden together with part of England, Ireland and North Germany.

Skóggangr

Outlaw. Literally "Forest-Walker". Exiled from society.

Skrälingi

"Weaklings"/"Cowards"; the Viking's name for the indigenous people in Vinland and Markland (in present day Canada).
Presumably Haudenosaunee (Iroquois). There is an island in Canada called Skraeling Island (latitude: 78° 52' 60 N,

longitude: 75° 55' 0 W) located on the east coast of Ellesmere Island in the Canadian territory of Nunavut.

Slave/Slavic

The ethnic groups in present day eastern Europe who have involuntarily given name to slave/slavery.

Sleipnir

Óðinn's eight-legged horse.

Snorri Sturluson

1179-1241

Icelandic chieftain, historian and writer. Wrote the Prose Edda.

Snøfrid Svåsedottir

Sámi princess, daughter to king Svåse, and married to Norwegian king Haraldr Hárfagri. She acted as one of his chief advisors, and according to legend had him under a spell. This is one of the very few examples of a Sámi playing a significant role in Viking history. The Saga of Snøfrid mentions that when she died her body was as fresh as if she'd been alive, for three years, while the king mourned her. This "sleeping beauty" might be the origin to the fairy tale Snow White. Snøfrid translates to "Snow-peace".

St. Brice's Day massacre

The St. Brice's Day massacre, that occurred 13th November 1002, was the mass killing of all Danes in England, ordered by King Æthelred the Unready in response to a perceived threat to his life.

Sturla Þórðarson

1214–1284

Nephew and pupil of the famous saga-writer Snorri Sturluson. He is best known for writing Íslendinga saga, the longest saga within Sturlunga saga, and Hákonar saga Hákonarsonar.

Svartálfheim

Home of the Svartálfr/Dvergr (Black Elves/Dwarfs), inside a mountain.

Svartálfr

Black elves, living in Svartálfheim, inside a mountain. They are not especially charming, but they can produce high quality stunningly beautiful items that holds magical powers, like Mjölnír and Brísingamen.

Svea

A North Germanic tribe who inhabited Svealand, around Lake Mälaren ("land of the Swedes"), in central Sweden and one of the progenitor groups of modern Swedes, along with Gautar and Gotar. They had their tribal centre in Gamla Uppsala. (Also see Rus and Varangian).

Sveinald Ingvarsson

943–972

Known as Sviatoslav the Brave, son of Ingvarr and Helga of Kyiv. Despite the fact that his mother with great gestures and bloodshed converted Kievan Rus to Christianity, and later became a saint in the Orthodox Church, Sviatoslav remained a pagan all his life. His decade-long reign over the Kievan Rus' was marked by rapid expansion into the Volga River valley, the Pontic steppe, and the Balkans. By the end of his short life, Sveinald carved out for himself the largest state in Europe. He was ambushed and slain by the Pechenegs in 972. The Chronicle reports that his skull was made into a chalice by the Pecheneg khan.

Sveinn "tjúguskegg" Haraldsson

963–1014

In English: Sweyn Forkbeard, in Danish: Svend Tveskæg. King of Denmark, Norway and England. Son of Haraldr "Blátǫnn" Gormsson, and father of Knútr "Ínn ríki" Sveinsson.

Svend Estridsen

1019–1076

Danish king, who had some luck in protecting the borders, but very little luck in expanding the kingdom. Instead he spend his time consolidating and further establishing the Christian church in Denmark, and even more time in bed – and not alone! He was married to Gyda Anundsdatter, Gunhild Sveinsdatter and Ellisiv of Kyiv (one at a time), and with them he had the sons Svend Korsfarer, Thrugils Svendsen and Knud Magnus. With various frills he had (hold on!): Harald Hen, Sigrid Svendsdatter, Knud den Hellige, Oluf Hunger, Ingerid Svendsdatter, Erik Ejegod, Benedikt Svendsen, Bjørn Svendsen, Svend Tronkræver, Guttorm Svendsen, Eymund Svendsen, Ubbe Svendsen, Niels Svendsen, Thorgils Svendsen, Ragnhild Svendsdatter and Helene Svendsdatter. That's 19 in all.

Sviatoslav den tapre

See Sveinald Ingvarsson

Sweyn Forkbeard

See Sveinn "tjúguskegg" Haraldsson.

Sæhrímnir

Sæhrímnir is the magical wild boar that is killed and eaten every night by the Æsir and Einherjar. Like all other creatures eaten in Ásgarðr it will appear whole the next day.

Tacitus

Roman writer who describes Scandinavia in the year 98 AD, in the book "Germania".

Þing

Decision-making and legislative assembly of free citizens (not slaves and children).

Þórr

Þórr ("Thor" or "Tor") is the Æsir for humans, and a son of Óðinn.

Þórr's most priced possession is no doubt his magical war hammer, Mjölnír (see that).

Þórr is the new kid on the block in Norse mythology, as there are no signs of him in archaeological digs from the bronze age.

Þórvi "Tanmark Bod" Haralðrsdottir

C. 900–950

Thýra Danebod, "Pride of Denmark", the first official queen of Denmark, and a huge power player in her own right. Married to Gormr "Gamli" Hardeknudsson (and gave him legitimacy) and mother of Haraldr "Blátǫnn" Gormsson. Mentioned on several runestones, and can be perceived as the actual ruler of Denmark as a kingdom. Þórvi means "Þórr's wife".

Trelleborg

A small city in southern Sweden, but also the name for several round castles build in Denmark and southern Sweden during the reign of Haraldr "Blátǫnn" Gormsson. These fortresses have a strictly circular shape, with roads and gates pointing in the four cardinal directions.

Tról

Trolls are a kind of jǫtunn that are exiled from Jotunheimr, and live in Miðgarðr. They seek solitude and can be dangerous if disturbed.

Trælle

Thralls, Slaves.

Týr

Týr is a warrior Æsir, along with Óðinn and Þórr.
The "T" rune (ᛏ) is often associated with him, and used to secure victory.
Tuesday is named after Týr.

Uppsala

The main religious (Forn Siðr) centre of Sweden. The temple at Uppsala contained magnificent idols of the main Æsir; Þórr, Óðinn and Freyr. Established around the year 300 AD, and now a vitally important archaeological site. Located 70 km north of Stockholm Uppsala is a thriving city, and home to the oldest – still active – university in Scandinavia, est. 1477.

Uppåkra

Swedish (formerly Danish) city, established c. 100 BC. Uppåkra declined and was possibly in part relocated to Lund in the 990s.

Útgarðar

Fortress in Jǫtunheimr, where the feared jǫtunn Út-garða-Loki presides. (Not to be confused with Loki)

Útlagi

Literally "Outlaw". Exiled from society.

Valdamarr Sveinaldsson

958–1015

Vladimir the Great. Born in 958, Valdemarr was the illegitimate and youngest son of Sveinald Ingvarrsson (Sviatoslav I of Kiev) by his housekeeper Malusha. Became the ruler of Kievan Rus in 980 after killing his two elder brothers.

Valhǫll

Valhal or Valhalla. A majestic hall located in Ásgarðr and presided over by Óðinn. Half of those who die in combat (Einherjar) enter Valhǫll, while the other half are chosen by the goddess Freyja to reside in Fólkvangr. The Einher-jar live in Valhǫll until Ragnarök when they will march out of its many doors to fight against the jǫtunn. It's an all-inclusive luxury battle training camp, only surpassed by Fólkvangr.

Valkyrja

Female figures who guide souls of the dead to Ásgarðr (Fólkvangr or Valhǫll). Mortally wounded warriors they finish off. In rare cases, they interfere in the fight.

Vanaheimr

Where the Vanir lives.

Vanir

A group of deities associated with fertility, wisdom, and the ability to see the future. The Vanir are one of two groups of deities (the other being the Æsir).

After the Æsir–Vanir War, the Vanir became a subgroup of the Æsir, and the Vanir Njörðr, Freyr and Freyja are send to Ásgarðr as hostages.

Varangian

Old Norse: Væringjar. Svea (see that)/Rus (see that) Viking conquerors, traders and settlers, mostly from present day Sweden.

The Varangian settled in the territories of modern day Belarus, Russia and Ukraine, and in the 9th century, they founded the medieval state of Kievan Rus (see that).

They also formed the Byzantine Varangian Guard (see that).

Varangian Garde

Viking Guard, an army of Rus (see that) Viking mercenaries in the service of the Byzantine Emperor.

Vegvisir

The Vegvisir (The Guide) is a magical symbol intended to help the bearer find their way home. The symbol is attested in the Huld Manuscript, collected in Iceland by Geir Vigfusson in 1860, and does not have any earlier attestations.

It's very popular as a tattoo motif among modern Vikings, though.

Vik

Cove

Viken

(Old Norse: Vík or Víkin) was the historical name during the Iron Age and the High Middle Ages for an area that originally surrounded the Oslo fjord and included the coast of Bohuslän. Its definition changed over time, and from the Middle Ages, Viken included only Bohuslän. The term Viking may derive from Vikin.

Vikingr

Expedition participant or raider.

Vikingu

Expedition.

Vili & Vé

Óðinn's two brothers.

Vinland

L'Anse aux Meadows in present day Canada. Maybe all of Gulf of Saint Lawrence.

Vladimir the Great

See Valdamarr Sveinaldsson

Vǫlsunga saga

The story about the rise and fall of the Vǫlsunga clan, written in the 1300s, but composed much earlier, and kept alive for hundreds of years in the oral skjalðe tradition.
The main character is Sigurdr Fáfnirsbane, and his name really says it all: Fáfnir is the name of a feared dragon, and ""bane"" means murderer.
One of the treasures Fáfnir is holding is the cursed golden ring Andvaranaut, that will help the owner find riches, but will eventually kill him.

Yes, the Vǫlsunga saga is the inspiration for both *Der Ring des Nibelungen* and *Lord of the Rings*.

This Saga contains everything you need from a story, including murders (plural), incestuous pregnancy, monsters, æsir, mysteries, gold, conspiracies and magic – including Óðinn sticking a sword in a tree, promising great powers to whomever can pull it out.

Sigurdr Fáfnirsbane leaves a daughter, the vǫlve Áslaug, which makes the Saga of Ragnarrs Sons picking up where Vǫlsunga saga ends.

Völve

Female shaman. Many years after the introduction of Christianity people would still consult a Völve, and when the church got sick and tired of the competition the witch-hunts in Scandinavia began (c. 1530).

Also read "Seiðr"."

Wends

Historical name for Slavs who inhabited present day north east Germany.

Yamnaya

The Yamnaya people originated in the Siberian steppes 7000 years ago, formed a herding and agricultural culture in the area north of the Black Sea (present day Ukraine), and invaded northern Europe in c. 3000 BC.

Blending with the much darker skinned locals they became the forefathers of the Slavic, Germanic, Celtic, Saxon, Dane (etc.) tribes.

This invasion simultaneously sparked the beginning of the Bronze Age.

Roughly speaking we can say that Europe was populated in three major waves: The hunter-gatherers from Africa

45000 years ago, the Anatolian farmers 9000 years ago, and the Yamnaya 5000 years ago.

The further north in Europe you go, the higher the percentage of Yamnaya DNA.

Yggdrasil

The world tree.

In pre-modern times, before the light pollution, you could see the canopy in the sky at night (as the Milky Way).

Ymir

The original creator of the world and all life.

Yngvarr Víðförli

?–1041

Ingvarr the far travelled, a Rus Viking from central Sweden who led a huge expedition to secure the Volga river, into Serkland (the Muslim world). No less than 26 runestones tell about this expedition, and people who died en route, and several sagas and chronicles mention his expedition, including the Georgian Chronicle.

York

See "Jórvik".

Ælla of Northumbria

815–867

King of Northumbria, in present day England. According to sagas he killed Ragnarr Loðbrók in a pit of snakes, and coursed the Great Heathen Army. According to the Saga of Ragnarr's Sons he was blood eagled, but according to The Anglo-Saxon Chronicle he died in the battlefield at York. Both can be right, depending on how we interpret Blood Eagle (see that).

Æsir

A group of deities in the Norse religion. The main characters, you might say. Mortal, but holds magic powers and
lives for thousands of years. Old Norse: áss or ǫss, plur.
æsir, femin. ásynja.

Æthelred the Unready

966–1016

Old Norse: Aðalráðr. In 1002, Æthelred ordered what
became known as the St. Brice's Day massacre of Danish
settlers. In 1013, King Sveinn "tjúguskegg" Haraldsson of
Denmark therefore invaded England, as a result of which
Æthelred fled to Normandy in 1013 and was replaced by
Sveinn.

TIMELINE

300	Uppsala established
536	Two major volcanic eruptions created a global period of cooling, often referred to as "three years without summer". The global death toll was enormous, and the event is now thought to be the origin of the myth of Fimbulvintr.
650	Ribe established
750	Birka established
780	Heiðabýr established
789	First recorded Viking raid in England (Dorset)
793	Lindisfarne raided
795	First recorded Viking raid in Ireland
795	First recorded Viking raid in Scotland
800	First Dane Viking settlement in Ireland
820	First recorded Viking raid in France
841	Dane Vikings founding Dublin
844	Dane Vikings Siege Seville, Al-Andalus (not successfully)
845	Dane Vikings siege Paris
850	Dane Vikings winter in England
860	Dane Vikings settle on Iceland
860	Rus Vikings attack Miklagarðr (Constantinople)
862	Rus Vikings establish kingdom in Holmgarðr (Novgorod)

865	The Great Heathen Army invade England
866	Dane Vikings establish kingdom in Jórvik (York)
879	Rus Vikings move capital from Holmgarðr to Kyiv, Kievan Rus is formally established
886	Treaty establishes Danelaw
911	Hrólfr is given a part of the Frankish kingdom and establish Normandy
941	Rus Vikings siege Miklagarðr (Constantinople)
944	Rus Vikings siege Miklagarðr (again)
981	Eiríkur "Rauði" Þorvaldsson discovers Greenland
986	Eiríkur "Rauði" Þorvaldsson establish Brattahlíð; settlement and trading station in Greenland
986	Bjarni Herjólfsson discovers Vinland (Canada)
1000	Leifur "Heppni" Eiríksson and his sister Freydís Eiríksdóttir establishes settlement in Vinland (Canada)
1000	(C.) Scandinavian countries officially declared Christian (Roman Catholic)
1000	Oslo (Viken) established
1009	Dane Vikings attack London
1015	Dane Vikings abandon settlement in Vinland
1016	Knútr "Ínn ríki" Sveinsson becomes king of England
1018	Knútr "Ínn ríki" Sveinsson becomes king of Denmark

1028   Knútr "Ínn ríki" Sveinsson becomes king of Norway

1049   Heiðabýr raided and burned by Haraldr "Harðráði" Sigurðarson

1066   King Harold Godwinson defeats Haraldr "Harðráði" Sigurðarson at the battle of Stamford Bridge

1066   King Harold Godwinson is defeated by Normandy Viking ruler William the Conqueror at the battle of Hastings. The beginning of 300 years of Normandy rule in England.

1103   Scandinavia's first archbishop, in Lund

1219   June 15th at the battle of Lindanäs in Estonia the Danish flag is introduced. According to legend it fell from the sky into the hands of the King. It's the first and oldest national flag in the world, and still in use.

1242   Kievan Rus conquered by Mongols

1397   The Kalmar Union is established between Denmark, Norway and Sweden, under the leadership of Danish Queen regnant Margrete Valdemarsdatter.

1453   Varangian Guard dismantled by the Ottoman invasion

1523   The Kalmar Union collapses

1530   (C.) Scandinavian countries reformed to Lutheran Christianity

1658   Roskildefreden; Denmark forced to give Skåne, Halland, Blekinge, Öland and Gotland to Sweden

1728   Denmark claims Greenland and establish colony

1808   The Finnish War was fought between Sweden and Russia from February 1808 to September 1809. As a result of the war, Finland which formed the eastern third of Sweden proper became the autonomous Grand Duchy of Finland within Imperial Russia.

1814   January 14th at the Treaty of Kiel, the king of Denmark-Norway ceded Norway to the king of Sweden. Denmark keeps Greenland, Faroe Islands and Iceland

1864   Denmark looses Slesvig-Holsten to Germany in a war

1873   The term "Viking Age" is invented

1876   Scenographer Carl Emil Doepler creates horned helmets for the first Bayreuther Festspiele production of Wagner's "Der Ring des Nibelungen"

1905   Norway independent

1917   Finland independent (from both Russia and Sweden)

1918   Even though Denmark was not partaking in World War one, Germany is forced to give North Slesvig to Denmark, after loosing the war. The area is renamed to Sønderjylland

1940   Denmark and Norway occupied by Nazi Germany

1941 US occupy Greenland with permission from the Danish ambassador in USA. He has gone rogue, since the Danish government is under Nazi German control. Occupation ends in 1945, but one military base remain in Thule.

1944 Iceland independent

1945 End of World War 2, occupation of Denmark and Norway ends

1945 Denmark (including. Greenland and Faroe Islands) and Norway joins United Nations

1946 Iceland and Sweden joins United Nations

1949 Denmark, Norway and Iceland becomes members of NATO

1955 Finland joins United Nations

1973 Denmark become EU member

1979 Greenland gained autonomy from Denmark, with some limitations. Leaves EU.

1995 Sweden and Finland become EU members

2023 Sweden and Finland applies for NATO membership

2023 Finland joins NATO

MEET:THE:VIKINGS

ONLINE

1000 Viking Facts By historian Anders Lundt Hansen
https://www.facebook.com/1000VikingFacts

Viking Archaeology
http://viking.archeurope.info/

Exact replicas from Viking jewellery in museums
https://museum-jewelry.com/

Science article about Viking DNA
https://videnskab.dk/kultur-samfund/
forsker-vikingerne-var-ikke-racerene-skandinaver

Rune Stone Database
https://www.runesdb.eu/

Rune Search Database
https://app.raa.se/open/runor/search

The Danish Forn Siðr Society
https://www.fornsidr.dk/

The Swedish Forn Siðr Society
https://asa-samfundet.se/

The Midgård Expedition
https://midgardexpedition.com/

The Anatomy of Viking Art
https://jonaslaumarkussen.com/

ICELAND

Key locations for Viking History in Iceland
https://www.visiticeland.com/article/
key-locations-for-viking-history-in-iceland

Horse riding tours with a Viking
https://mriceland.is/

NORWAY

Link to the best Viking experiences and exhibitions
https://www.visitnorway.no/aktiviteter-og-attraksjoner/
kunst-kultur/vikinger/norges-beste-vikingopplevelser

Lofotr Viking Museum
https://www.lofotr.no/

Draken Harald Hårfagre Viking Ship
https://www.drakenhh.com/

DENMARK

Danish National Museum
https://natmus.dk/

Danish Viking Ship Museum
https://www.vikingeskibsmuseet.dk/

Trelleborg (Viking fortress) in Denmark
https://natmus.dk/museer-og-slotte/trelleborg

Viking Exhibition in Ribe
https://www.ribevikingecenter.dk/

Link to 13 Danish Viking Exhibitions

https://www.visitdenmark.dk/danmark/oplevelser/kulturoplevelser/13-danske-vikingeattraktioner

Viking Open Air Theatre

https://www.vikingespil.dk/

SWEDEN

Birka Viking Village

https://www.birkavikingastaden.se/

Uppsala Viking Museum

https://www.upplandsmuseet.se/gamla-uppsala-museum

Trelleborgen (the Viking fortress) in Trelleborg

https://www.trelleborg.se/uppleva-gora/kultur/trelleborgen

The Viking Museum in Stockholm

https://thevikingmuseum.com/

SUOMI (FINLAND)

Rosala Viking Centre

https://rosala.fi/

GERMANY

Haithabu (Hedeby) Viking Centre

https://haithabu.de/

GREENLAND

Vikings in Greenland
https://visitgreenland.com/things-to-do/
vikings-in-greenland

CANADA

Vikings in Canadian History Museum
https://www.historymuseum.ca/vikings

L'Anse aux Meadows National Historic Site
https://www.newfoundlandlabrador.com/top-destinations/
lanse-aux-meadows

UNITED KINGDOM

Jorvik Viking Centre
https://www.jorvikvikingcentre.co.uk/

ÉIRE (IRELAND)

Dublinia – Dublin Viking Museum
https://www.dublinia.ie/

FRANCE

Viking adventures at Parc Ornavik (Normandy)
https://en.normandie-tourisme.fr/
viking-adventures-parc-ornavik

THE SAGA CONTINUES

VIKINGR.SITE

9 788879 740248 1